Life of a Smuggler: Fact and Fiction

Tom

Have a Very Happy
Birthday !

4 November 2021

With very best wishes

Granpa Tim

For John Fitzhugh Millar of Newport
House, Williamsburg.
He would have made a fine
eighteenth-century Rhode Island
'Gentleman'!

Life of a Smuggler: Fact and Fiction

Helen Hollick

PEN & SWORD
HISTORY

AN IMPRINT OF PEN & SWORD BOOKS LTD.
YORKSHIRE – PHILADELPHIA

First published in Great Britain in 2019 by
Pen and Sword History
An imprint of
Pen & Sword Books Ltd
Yorkshire - Philadelphia

ISBN 9781526727138

Typeset in India By IMPEC e Solutions

Printed and bound in the United Kingdom By CPI

Pen & Sword Books Ltd incorporates the Imprints of Pen & Sword Books
Archaeology, Atlas, Aviation, Battleground, Discovery, Family History,
History, Maritime, Military, Naval, Politics, Railways, Select, Transport, True
Crime, Fiction, Frontline Books, Leo Cooper, Praetorian Press, Seaforth
Publishing, Wharncliffe and White Owl.

For a complete list of Pen & Sword titles please contact

PEN & SWORD BOOKS LIMITED
47 Church Street, Barnsley, South Yorkshire, S70 2AS, England
E-mail: enquiries@pen-and-sword.co.uk
Website: www.pen-and-sword.co.uk

or

PEN AND SWORD BOOKS
1950 Lawrence Rd, Havertown, PA 19083, USA
E-mail: Uspen-and-sword@casematepublishers.com
Website: www.penandswordbooks.com

Contents

SMUGGLERS!

Five and twenty ponies,
Trotting through the dark –
Brandy for the Parson, 'Baccy for the Clerk.
Laces for a lady; letters for a spy,
Watch the wall my darling while the Gentlemen go by!

' Gentlemen'? Were smugglers really gentlemen? Samuel Johnson published his Dictionary of the English Language in 1755 and described the smuggler as: 'A wretch who, in defiance of justice and the laws, imports or exports goods as either contraband or without payment of the customs.' It seems he was not impressed by the Gentlemen Free Traders.

On the other side of the coin, the eighteenth century economist and supporter of Free Trade, Adam Smith, proclaimed: 'The smuggler is a person who ... would have been in every respect an excellent citizen had not the laws of his country made that a crime which nature never meant to be so.'

All well and good, except many smugglers committed violence – and even murder.

Smuggling. The very word conjures an image of a quiet moonlit night, a tall ship rocking gently at anchor out in a slightly wind-ruffled bay and men wearing three-cornered hats making their swift, but silent, way along remote West Country lanes that zigzag between high banks and thick, foxglove and cow-parsley-strewn hedgerows. The men are leading a string of pack ponies tied nose to tail, their hooves muffled by rough sacking. On the ponies' backs are casks of brandy or kegs of tobacco… But is that how smuggling really happened?

In reality, smuggling is the illegal importation of goods – be they mercantile, narcotic substances, migrating people or secret information. The two motivations being to avoid paying tax and to make a profit, the latter being the ultimate goal, somewhere along the line, for those involved with breaking the law by smuggling. The smugglers of the past would argue against that. They bought and paid for the goods which they intended to smuggle, so these were not stolen items. The contraband was transported, carried and delivered at the smugglers' own expense and in their own time, so there was nothing illegal there. The items were in high demand by the majority of the population, many of whom could not afford to purchase them legally – and we are not talking luxury goods, much of the smuggled contraband were essentials, such as salt, tin, leather and corn. The smugglers' conviction was that to not pay government duties on prohibited goods was justified because of a right to buy or sell with the freedom of choice, unrestricted by laws. After all, the only ones who suffered from the effects of smuggling (leaving aside the unsavoury aspect of violence where organised gangs were concerned) was the government because of uncollected taxes. Few of us would lose much sleep about that small fact!

Unfortunately, rogues and ruffians often corrupt the subtle bending of the law to new extremes of criminality. What started with the relatively harmless smuggling of everyday items by a small group of villagers and fisher-folk was swept aside by viciousness, bloody battles, torture and murder. Alas, derring-do romantic rebels the majority of smugglers were not.

Our imagined view of smuggling and smugglers, like most romantic illusions and ideals of the past (or even the present, come to that) originate from Hollywood, TV and novels. We envision the handsome Errol Flynn-type rogue pitting his wits against authority, almost losing his life into the bargain, but always ending up in love with the pretty, heaving-bosomed, blonde-haired girl.

From these perceived images we see the brave smuggler wearing a merry grin, probably a tooth or two missing, and sharp miss-nothing eyes. Maybe he is a bit rough around the edges and coarse in manner and language, but he is also a God-fearing man who can use his fists or his cudgel if he has to, but has honourable and loyal intentions.

Fiction and poetry have heightened these myths: *Moonfleet*, *Jamaica Inn* and Rudyard Kipling's *A Smuggler's Song*, probably more well known as *Watch The Wall My Darling*, or *As The Gentlemen Go By*, have been much loved for many years. Kipling's talent for turning emotion, imagination and the excitement of adventure into prose and poetry comes to the fore in his poem. Despite its romantic lilt it sums up the more accurate truth of the smuggler and his secretive, nocturnal occupation. Its words and underlying meaning fit the facts behind smuggling far more than any Hollywood movie.

Even so, the average smuggler of the seventeenth and eighteenth centuries was very far from Kipling's poetic view or the perceived Big Screen heroic image.

Chapter One

Romantic Rebels?
Or Despicable Thieves?

Little Known Fact:
The word 'smuggle' probably entered the English
language in the 1600s

The first question, although maybe not the most obvious, is where does the word 'smuggle' come from?

'Smuggler' was a general term the same as 'thief' or 'crook'. 'To Smuggle' as with many of our nautical-based words, comes from Low German 'schmuggeln', or the Dutch, 'smokkelen', both of which have an original meaning of something like 'to transport illegally'. It is believed that the word 'smuggle' entered into the English language during the 1600s, possibly during the era when the eldest son of Charles I, himself to become crowned as Charles II, was in exile with many of his supporters in the Netherlands. One of his assistants was Samuel Pepys, of the Diary fame, whose day job was to oversee various organisation policies of the Royal Navy. He would have kept a sharp eye on any illicit trading, although I would wager he occasionally took advantage of anything offered at a reasonable price – no questions asked. During the rage of the Great Fire of London in 1666, one of the things he buried in case the fire spread to his house, was a parcel of expensive cheese. French Brie, Devon Blue or Cornish Yarg perhaps? (My favourite cheeses!) Master Pepys, however, preferred to bury his Italian Parmesan.

Smugglers did not call themselves 'smugglers'. The 'Trade' could be associated with gentlemen, bootleggers, contrabandists, moonshiners, rum runners and traffickers among other general descriptions. Smugglers were not merely the men who brought illicit cargo ashore and hurried it away on the backs of ponies. The term could apply to almost anyone involved in obtaining goods illegally: from the thug with his heavy cudgel protecting an inbound cargo, to the local squire who financed the deal or supplied the ship and horses to transport the goods.

What are some smuggling terms? (Or, when is a donkey not a donkey!)

Bill of Landing: a shipmaster's receipt detailing the cargo.
Boiled Man: someone who has bribed the excise men to be left alone.
Bit of red: a soldier.
Chatter broth: tea.
Composition: a fine for smuggling, calculated according to the value of goods seized and the smuggler's financial status.
Cousin Jacky: brandy.
Creeping: the act of dragging the seabed to recover temporarily hidden contraband.
Creeping irons: grappling irons or hooks used for creeping.
Crop: a cargo of contraband.
Darks: moonless nights.
Donkey: a one-legged stool used by coastguards. In later years called a shooting stick.
Drawback: the official refund of excise duty.
Dry Goods: non-liquid contraband.
Funt: a smuggler's warning light.
Genever: gin.
Guineaboat: a fast galley used for carrying guineas to France.
Hollands: Dutch gin.
Rummage: to search, especially for contraband.
Run: a smuggling operation.
Sowing the crop: sinking contraband in the sea with weights and markers in order to hide it.

Stinkibus: spirits which have gone off after prolonged submersion in the sea.

Tub: a small cask, flat on one side, oval on the other. Used in pairs to be carried by 'tubmen'.

Vizard: a cloth facemask worn across the mouth and nose.

Working the crop: recovering sunken casks that have been temporarily hidden in the sea.

Even if you do muddle a real donkey and a stool – you can sit on both!

Smuggling in England, from earliest times to the mid–eighteenth century, affected the population of almost every large city, bustling town and rural village alike. In its wake came claims, by rich merchants, that distress was being caused to legitimate workers by depleting the income of respectable traders from the most successful shopkeeper to the lowest stallholder. Importing contraband was rife almost everywhere along the coastal waters, and included the lawmakers and law enforcers as the men who undertook smuggling. If caught, prior to the later eighteenth century, smugglers were likely to be dealt lenient sentences as many a magistrate relied on contraband to replenish his own stock of brandy or tobacco. From high-class rich men to the lowest of the poor, smuggling was a part of daily life for governors, military and naval officers, local squires, the landed gentry, members of Parliament and the clergy – very few men and women did not have their fingers in this lucrative pie. Or should that be barrel?

It is estimated that as much as half of the alcohol consumed throughout England in the mid-eighteenth century was smuggled in by various notorious gangs. They were virtually unopposed as the coasts and estuaries were rarely guarded, let alone patrolled. Not until the late 1700s did the excise men, backed by local militia troops, start being effective.

A booklet, *Advice to the Unwary*, published in 1780 details the consequence to the economy brought about by smuggling. The unknown author explains that silk weavers could not compete with cheap, illegally imported silks. He adds to his (convincing?) argument that were the smugglers to turn their attention to legitimate fishing, they would be of more use to their communities. Some of the same old misunderstandings regarding the out-of-work and the poor do not change do they? Included in this tirade is the fact that imported genever (gin) was adding to the problem of alcoholism, something that William Hogarth also depicted in his highly detailed (and often amusing) satirical caricatures of the depravities of London's citizens. The author's words were a forlorn cry, however, as many individuals looked to the money in their pockets, not caring, beyond a cursory shrug, about the poor and destitute. The author's aim was to inform the public and bring the smugglers to justice. A wasted rant, for smuggling continues to this day carried out by the holidaymaker hoping to sneak a bottle of Scotch through the 'nothing to declare' lane at the airport. And there are still professional smugglers bringing in high-grade drugs via various routes.

In 1724, the author of novels and political pamphlets (and castaway sailors), Daniel Defoe, wrote about Lymington in Hampshire on the English south coast: 'I do not find they have any foreign commerce, except it be what we call smuggling and roguing; which I may say, is

Twenty-first century Customs & Excise! (©Monika Wisniewska)

the reigning commerce from the mouth of the Thames to the Land's End in Cornwall.'

Some tales of smuggling exploits have been passed down through local legend – the *Battle of Sidley Green* (as we will find out) is one example, although how many tales have been exaggerated to become believed fact, we can only speculate.

Annoyingly for writers of fiction or informative textbooks, there is a marked absence of facts recorded about smuggling. The trouble with secretive activities – they remained secret. Most of the knowledge we have gleaned today is from archived newssheets, both local and national, from letters and reports penned by revenue officers safely stored, again in archives, or from court records. These snippets of information give only the bare facts and intriguing names, with maybe an occupation listed alongside. They are also only about those smugglers who were caught, tried and sentenced (or reprieved). There is an enormous lack of evidence and information about the clever smugglers. The ones we do not know about; those who did not get caught. It is these mysterious men who have given us the romantic concept of their lives, glossing over the fact that in reality they were rebels against law and order, and were nothing short of thieves defrauding the government of revenue.

WHEN?

Chapter Two

From Medieval to Modern

When did smuggling start? Smuggling – the 'Free Trade' – reached its height in the seventeenth and eighteenth centuries, peaking in the early 1800s, which is the era we think of for our image of the Free Traders, but importing goods, whatever they were, illegally and under the noses of law enforcement officers and tax gatherers was nothing new…

Little Known Fact:
The term 'Customs and Excise' came from paying a customary toll on imported wine at selected ports in the late tenth century.

Tolls were imposed on wine imports by the Anglo-Saxon king, Æthelred II (966–1016) his name meaning 'noble-counselled', but was soon changed to Æthelred Unraed – 'ill-counselled', which then became corrupted to 'Unready'. When he desperately needed money (Danegeld) to pay for holding off the invading Danes, led by Sven Forkbeard and his son Cnut (King Canute of holding back the tide fame), he invented the idea of 'tax' via import duty to be paid on bringing foreign wine into England. This was a clever way to raise funds: in order to continue trading, vintners had to surrender a portion of their cargo, and therefore their profit. Paying the enforced toll soon became a 'custom'. There is an old Frankish saying that doing something twice makes it a custom as binding as a law. These 'Custom Tolls', however, only applied to specific ports, so to land wine at an exempt harbour was not illegal. Of course, this meant that the wine traders used any port or harbour except the toll ports, although that entailed carting barrels of wine across country, which was neither cheap nor easy to do, so rather defeated the object. It is extraordinary what lengths people will go to in an attempt to avoid paying tax!

In England, smuggling contraband, as we think of it, started to become an annoying problem in the thirteenth century after King Edward I created his unpopular concept for a customs collection system in 1275. Smuggling in the 1200s had tended to lean towards exported goods rather than those imported, wool and hides in particular, both of which carried a high tax in order to finance various expensive wars. The wool business was one of England's most profitable trades, making the kingdom one of the wealthiest in the known world. But grain, especially when there was an embargo between England and what is now Europe (although, usually confined to France and/or Spain), for one reason or another was a lucrative smuggler's choice. Grain export was regularly prohibited because of concerns that the price would rise, thereby causing a shortage and then a famine which would, in turn, escalate to riots and unrest. The simple answer of not fighting lengthy and unnecessary wars did not seem to have occurred to anyone.

Romney Marsh sheep – essential for the Owlers and wool smuggling. (©Sixpixx)

Those early days of smuggling in the pre-fourteenth centuries were relatively hassle-free, for only the ports, harbours and estuaries were patrolled by revenue cutters, leaving elsewhere along coasts, creeks or rivers unguarded. But even secretive landings were not regarded as necessary, for it was simpler to pay the customs officers to look away. Poor pay meant that honest officials were as rare as unicorns.

Smuggling was successful because of the law-enforcers' inability to uphold the law. The revenue officers faced an almost hopeless task, at least until they eventually improved efficiency, increased their numbers and were able to do their job properly, assisted by rigid enforcement of the law of the land. Although, even then, smuggling persisted. Smuggling, for all its romantic imagery, however, evolved around sharp-witted opportunists who saw a way of getting rich quickly and easily. Go into any airport lounge today and you will see the customs men and women on patrol. Watching every move behind the scenes will be the dedicated staff monitoring the CCTV cameras. They know how to spot the covert glances, the sweating brow, that strange bulge, that peculiar limp.

The advantage, maybe even the comfort, of having them there is that they are not only alert for the modern smuggler, intent on outwitting Her Majesty's Revenue and Customs, but they are also doing their best to protect us from potential terrorists, and for that, despite our grumbles about import duty, we profoundly thank them.

As early as the mid-1520s, smuggling was a large-scale, organised business, especially for raw wool and corn. (Grain: rye, wheat, barley etc., is termed as 'corn' in the UK. It does not refer to the US corn-on-the-cob.) The government of the day introduced the necessity to hold a licence to export grain, a short-sighted move as legalities rarely bothered smugglers, particularly when such licences were expensive to obtain and added about fifty per cent to the price of corn. Much simpler to not bother with a licence and smuggle the corn in.

Some of the commercial records for the export trade from the South West's busy port of Bristol indicate that the illegal export of goods could have been a substantial portion of the city's actual trade, with smugglers making as much as 150 per cent profit on exporting grain, and eighty per cent for leather. It can be difficult to imagine that the river Avon today, trundling along between the city and the Severn Estuary, a distance of about six miles, was once a densely packed trade route for shipping, and a busy stretch of water for smuggling. Shipping masters would declare their legal cargoes loaded at the Bristol wharves, sail downriver to Avonmouth, and en route, meet with river-savvy bargemen offering extra, illegal, cargo.

Small-scale illegal importation of goods escalated rapidly during the 1600 and 1700s, and by 1800 was a vast and profitable industry, flooding the southern and eastern counties of England with contraband. One trip alone could bring in up to 3,000 gallons of brandy or gin. Equate this with a modern purchase of a case of twelve bottles of wine, which is heavy to carry and transport. Multiply the twelve-bottle box to over 1,000 cases. How would you bring it secretly into England? Where would you store it? How would you distribute it? Maybe this is one reason why smugglers are admired; such highly organised and executed operations require a certain amount of respect!

Little Known Fact:
There was so much cheap gin being smuggled into England that it was used as a household cleaner!

At times, there was such a glut of duty-free gin imported that housewives and servants along the Kent coast used it to clean their windows. As an aside, soak your jewellery, especially rings, in a small amount of gin. It brings the sparkle out most handsomely. Tea was another worthwhile commodity to smuggle. Almost half of all cuppas consumed in the 1700s and 1800s were brewed from smuggled tea.

In addition to the stealth of getting a cargo off-loaded and safely ashore, the contraband had to be purchased in the first place – the initial point of sale was not a freebie, 'Buy One Get One Free' supermarket special. Villagers and communities, if there were no rich gentleman financier to hand, would club together using every farthing available to purchase suitable goods. With the expectation of a decent profit reward, of course. No wonder the revenue and excise men were feared and hated; no wonder men, and women, took up weapons to protect their investment, or in some cases, forcibly claim back a confiscated cargo.

Like the traffic wardens of today, the revenue men and women of the past were only doing their job, but have usually been universally despised for it. From Early Medieval times when Æthelred, the Saxon king, introduced what he thought was a good way to make money in order to pay the Vikings to go away, to the controversial proposed laws of Brexit, smugglers have pitted their wits against the law enforcers, and have been, on the whole, applauded for their efforts by the ordinary people who prefer not to pay the high price of import duty.

WHY?

Chapter Three

To Pay or Not to Pay?
That Tricky Matter of Tax

The fewer restrictions on import or exports, the less smuggling there is. That is a fact for today and for the past. But civil war, war with France, or war with the American Colonists who were determined on pursuing independence from the king and British Government, needed financing. Placing taxation duty on mercantile goods was a way to raise funds. But to do so was extremely unpopular. So the question, 'why did smugglers smuggle?' is probably self-explanatory, but not necessarily so…

Apart from acquiring items that were needed at a bargain cost, smuggling was all about getting one over on the law, king, queen, government, revenue men and customs officials. From the Early Medieval days, when taxes were first introduced on imported and exported goods, those acquainted with the sea sought ways to circumnavigate paying extra tax. We think of the expensive or illegal items as the trading commodities of the smuggler – drugs, ivory, jewels – but in the past it was the everyday stuff that the smuggler's favoured, the brandy and the 'baccy (tobacco), wool, salt, leather and lace. If the government taxed it, the smugglers smuggled it.

There is an estimate that at least half of the smuggled brandy and about one-quarter of the tea brought into England came in via the rugged and remote coasts of Devon and Cornwall, with Romney Marsh giving the West Country a run for its money where ease of access and isolation was concerned. In the eighteenth century many goods which seem odd to us today as items worth smuggling carried a high import or export duty. Tea, for instance, could be purchased in France for about 7*d* lb, but sold in England at 5*s* lb. Tobacco could cost 2*s* 6*d* (roughly about £8 in modern equivalent UK sterling), with gin and brandy at £1 for a tub, but sold at £4 in its raw, undiluted state. More profit would be made once watered down. An average wage for a farm worker in the late 1700s would be between five to eight shillings a week – £24 if that was today's money. Tea, tobacco, brandy, spices, lace, were luxury goods, well beyond the affordability of the poor. Smuggling, therefore, was a way of affording items too expensive to buy elsewhere. And for the smuggler, it was a very profitable business investment.

Why the risk? There will always be enterprising people willing to supply a demand, and as many willing people to carry and sell the goods that are wanted – if to do so is financially worth taking the risk of being caught and punished. The source payments can be low, easy to-come-by cheap goods from across the English Channel. The actual smuggling can be relatively easy via a quiet cove, using a suitable boat and experienced seamen. The saleable price is always much higher than the outlay, but less than the carried taxation duties, resulting in an easy-made, welcome profit. Which is why the smugglers of our past history risked the chance of being arrested – and hanged – for smuggling. In some cases, even today, the risk is still worth taking.

The demand for expensive goods at a cheap price applied to all classes and all places, from the poor to the rich, from the slums of London to the remotest villages of the West Country. In the United States it is reckoned that more alcohol was consumed during the 1920s Prohibition than before or after that somewhat senseless, and as it turned out, useless, law. Drug smuggling has become a problem for many countries, and the call to legalise drugs in the UK, and thus put the smugglers and dealers effectively out of business, is an ongoing, if debatable solution.

By smuggling contraband into (or out of) a country, whatever the cargo may be, wherever it may originate, there was no export or import duty to pay. The goods could be transported without much fuss then sold on cheap, with a suitable profit added for the supplier's pocket and no questions asked. Smuggling, while not necessarily the means to 'get rich quick' was (is!) a way of making easy money, and, for those on a low income, making a meagre penny or pound stretch further.

Prior to the 1800s, the collection of duty by the government's various representatives was haphazard and poorly organised because the bureaucratic system for collecting it remained based on the ideas of the thirteenth century, which involved specific customs houses located at ports and harbours and was geared to the exportation of the wool trade. There was nothing efficient set in place to cover other items. With very few government officials or men of the military to patrol the many miles of British coastland, plus all the isolated coves and inlets, and with large numbers of men and women only too pleased to outwit king and country, smuggling became an everyday occupation among seafaring and coastal folk.

By the mid-1700s few coastal villages with secluded coves or beaches nearby, and within easy sailing distance of Europe, were smuggler-free. The Trade was more profitable than fishing – which had its use by providing a suitable and legitimate 'cover'. Small-time smuggling was rife, nearly everyone with opportunity did it, from bringing in small bundles of lace to a couple of kegs of French brandy. To sail to France, collect a legitimate cargo, with the addition of something illegal neatly hidden away, was easy to do because there was virtually no one to stop the enterprise of the Free Trade. There were very few customs officers, and those few often turned a blind eye – for a suitable reward. Once smuggling became a large scale business, however, the romantic notion of strolling ashore, unnoticed, with something to sell for profit tucked under your arm became just that – a romantic notion.

Getting caught was the main risk. Prior to the nineteenth century reform of the death penalty any thief, be he (or she) a child stealing a loaf of bread, an older brother poaching a rabbit, a woman stealing a gentleman's purse or a father smuggling in a few packets of tobacco, the sentence was the same: hanging.

Informants were a risk, especially where larger towns and busy inns were concerned. In small community villages where an unknown face roused suspicion, everyone knew everyone else and knew each other's business, so tattling was rare. Towns, and the growth of cities such as London and Bristol, then Sheffield, Manchester and Birmingham once the Industrial Revolution took hold, were places where strangers came and went, and where there was little loyalty between individual families – or even within families.

The other dangers to face a smuggler were natural ones; the sea can be a harsh mistress, storms can blow up within moments, boats can be damaged or sink. No wife or mother could ever take it for granted that her husband or son would return safe from the sea, be it for a legitimate fishing trip or a smuggling run.

Not all of the dangers were for the smugglers. Where people are involved their lives could also be at risk. Illegal immigration is another worldwide concern today, especially where people-trafficking of women and children for the sex-trade is concerned. It is reasonable to understand why people living in desperate situations – war, famine or under a cruel regime of dictatorship tyranny – are willing to risk all to pay the people-smugglers to help them. But at what cost? The difference between smuggling people and people trafficking is small, but simple. A smuggler assists people to enter (illegally) a country of safety for a fee, on arrival they are free to do as they will. Trafficking involves victims who think they are heading for a better life, ending up in a worse situation than they started out, usually enforced into slavery or sex-working, and kept by coercion, threats, fraud, deception and plain bullying, with little hope of escape.

There are, therefore, two sides to 'people smuggling'. The insidious and abhorrent exploitation of the innocent and vulnerable, especially of young women and children, and smuggling frightened, impoverished families from war-torn or military-controlled areas rife with fear and danger in order to seek a better life. Both are illegal, the first stomach-churningly nasty, the second, understandable – were it not for the money-grabbing motivation of the people-smugglers who have no regard for those who are trying to escape the horrors of their lives. Sadly, many of these poor people die in their desperate attempt.

People smuggling, however, was not always so insidious. Both factual and fictional history shows these attempts at seeking freedom or safety in a better light. When slavery was legal in North America, many African slaves managed to escape via the Underground Railroad which provided secret trails up through the Rocky Mountains to

Canada. Similarly, many of Jewish faith were smuggled from the Nazi occupied territories to safety during the Second World War. So not all people smuggling is a bad thing.

Little Known Fact:
The English Civil Wars between King and Parliament was the direct cause of raised import and export tax – which in turn led to a rise in smuggling contraband.

The seventeenth century English Civil War, which was not one continuous war, but a series of escalating disputes on and off the battlefield between king and government (although in reality Catholic against anti-Catholic), resulted in the public execution of King Charles I in January 1649, followed by a dictatorship rule by Oliver Cromwell. The king's son, Prince Charles, then the uncrowned King Charles II, fled into exile for about ten years, but was recalled to reign in 1660 after the Protectorate fell apart when Cromwell died. The English Parliament granted Charles II an income of over £1 million – today that would be not far short of £192 million – to run his kingdom, the majority of the money coming from customs and excise duty. The amount was nowhere near enough, so more taxes were added … and cleverly circumnavigated by the smugglers.

The Crown had, for many centuries, claimed a financial levy from all goods being brought into England. By 1688, however, the duties on imported goods was restructured in order to generate a higher income for the government treasury. Coffee, chocolate, tea, cider, beer and alcoholic spirits were taxable items, with other 'essentials' added and taxed, items which included soap.

As the Exchequer's slice of the cake progressively grew larger, sometimes in small amounts, sometimes in large chunks, depending on the fluctuations of numerous conflicts, so the necessity to smuggle became more imperative – and lucrative. By the mid-1700s the tea tax had risen by seventy per cent compared to the years prior to the English Civil War.

So who benefited? Crown and government yielded more tax income, but smuggled goods were in higher demand, and so more people turned to the Free Trade. No one likes to pay tax, especially for mercantile goods. Raise the level of taxes – or introduce them in the first place – and it is a forgone conclusion that people will try to avoid paying that tax. But outfoxing the officials by the use of wit and cunning was also part of the pleasure of smuggling.

WHO?

Chapter Four

Lone Fisherman or Organised Gang?

We have an idea that the smugglers were a handful of poor fisher-folk struggling to survive the harsh drudge of life as the major culprits. The notorious fictional characters that spring to mind are either drunkards, like the highly unpleasant Joss Merlyn from Daphne du Maurier's novel *Jamaica Inn*, or curmudgeonly old Jud Paynter from Winston Graham's *Poldark* books and TV series. 'Tidn't fair… tidn't proper…!' as Jud would remark.

Alternatively, our fictional perception of a typical smuggler is the handsome hero, quick to smile, pleasant mannered, a gentleman, a Robin Hood-like character.

Or maybe first to come to mind would be an opera? Based on a novel by Prosper Mérimée, Bizet's *Carmen*, which most people think of as a story of bullfighting, toreadors and Spanish ladies dressed in fabulously coloured flamenco dresses, actually revolves around smuggling. So who were the smugglers …?

Our perceived notion of a lone, crafty smuggler from a rural coastal village is not quite right. In fact, entire communities were involved in smuggling contraband of whatever nature or value. During the 1600–1800s nearly everyone who lived in or near an isolated fishing village along the south and West Country coasts of England, was involved, one way or another, with smuggling.

At the physical side of smuggling would be the poorer classes. Brain for the organising; brawn for the unloading, hauling and carting. These latter people would not be full-time smugglers; maybe a one-off, maybe taking part in several 'runs' a year. In between, they pursued an honest trade: fishermen, riverboat men, harbour pilots, but also bakers, cordwainers, blacksmiths, tavern landlords, merchants, storekeepers…. Others would perhaps store smuggled goods – anyone with a suitable cellar was deemed useful.

Kegs, bales, casks, baskets, barrels, were all brought in by sailing ships, usually anchored offshore, transferred to small rowing boats, then manhandled ashore, loaded on to pack ponies, mules or donkeys, put into carts or merely carried away in 'tubs' strapped to a man's chest and back. Sometimes, cargo had to be hauled up steep cliffs, hefted over banks of shingle, or taken along hidden pathways traversing wet marshland or open moors. And by night when there was no full moon. The idea of shadowy figures on a beach in the light of a full moon is fictional.

Entire communities of villagers were involved – smuggling was no longer a small-time business. When the preventative men eventually put a more effective effort into stopping smuggling, entire families were wiped out through starvation.

Little Known Fact:
Vicars were among the highest receivers of smuggled brandy and wine!

However, the brains and financing behind the runs were literate and educated well-to-do chaps – and sometimes chapesses! Landowners, tradesmen, businessmen. governors, Members of Parliament and magistrates – the very people who should be upholding the law not going against it. Even vicars were involved! Several good reverends are listed on surviving tally sheets as purchasers of smuggled contraband. 'Brandy for the Parson' in Kipling's poem is no made-up convenient rhyme. The parson enjoyed the benefit of smuggled tea and wine, the squire enjoyed his pipe of smuggled tobacco and glass of smuggled brandy – with French lace and exotic spices to keep the wife or mistress happy.

Nor were all smugglers Englishmen. Ports were busy places, especially the bigger harbours of London, Bristol, Falmouth, Weymouth and so forth. Race, colour and creed of all nations would have thronged the wharves and taverns as sailors, stevedores, prostitutes, ne'er-do-wells and down-and-outs. Some caution may

Friend or foe? Smuggler or blockade man? (©John Gomez)

have been taken with any foreigners or American Colonials during times of war, but did the pubs and brothels really care who frequented them? As long as the individual paid their silver, and secretively had a package of something worthwhile tucked in his pocket....

Narrowing it down, however, the seafarers who brought cargoes in (or out) of England were experienced sailors; fishermen or crew aboard wherries, coasters or riverboats. They knew about sailing, navigation, tides and currents. Knew the best places to bring goods ashore. On land, the smugglers were those who knew the secretive trails, where to hide and store contraband, the quickest, safest, routes to a final destination. At the top of the ladder, the richer folk provided the financing and the equipment.

Dorset's Lyme Regis Court records show a variety of trades for some of the landsmen – and women – who were caught and tried for smuggling:

Basket maker	Moses Cousins
Bricklayer	William Trim
Butcher	Robert Hatton
Cooper	James Ford
Dressmaker	Maria Bagwell
Ferryman	George Dowall
Innkeeper	George Kearley
Labourer	Thomas Zeally
Miller	William Oxford
Needlewoman	Ann Gummer
Shoemaker	William Powell

From lord to landowner, from magistrate to miller, very few did not, one way or another, have an interest in smuggled goods.

What were some of the 'terms of the trade'?

Batman (not the superhero!): A smuggler armed with a bat to protect the men bringing contraband ashore.

Boatman: hired to help crew a boat during a 'run'.

Contraband: any illegally imported goods.

Flaskers: men who specialised in liquor smuggling: rum, brandy, genever (gin) and such.

Free trader: what smugglers called themselves.

The tubmen would walk miles by night to deliver their barrels of brandy or gin.
(© Mia Pelletier)

Gentlemen: any smuggler.

Glutman: extra men used when and where required.

Landers: men who were in charge of organising where and how a cargo was to be brought ashore, and for arranging land–based networks for distributing contraband.

Owlers: derived from their night–time activities. 'Owling' came to be the term for wool smugglers. Wool smuggling was illegal from 1367 to

1824, but this specific term does not appear to have been used until the end of the 1600s.

Rum Runners: mostly associated with the Caribbean; rum smugglers.

Spotsman: the captain of a boat who could navigate to a designated drop-off point, even in the dark.

Tubmen: strong men with the ability to walk far and fast at night, taking contraband spirits away in small barrels called half-ankers – wooden 'tubs' strapped together in pairs and slung one across the chest, one behind the shoulders.

Venturer: a smuggler's financial backer.

Wreckers: men who deliberately lured ships on to rocks in order to steal the cargo.

Or did they? Read on…

Were ships deliberately wrecked in order to steal the cargo they carried?

Traditional legends claim that ships were lured by false lights and bonfires on to the rocks along the coasts of Devon and Cornwall. Waiting for the ship to founder and break up would be ruthless men eager to steal what they could of what would be brought ashore by the tide. Not strictly smuggling, but wrecking still involved the illegal and sinister side of bringing ashore untaxed cargo and taking it away for personal use or selling it for profit. Either way, it still meant that customs duty was not paid.

Many a movie or novel has the excitement, and horror, of this dreadful practice, but, sorry to disappoint, there is no evidence to support such tales and legends. Like so many exaggerations in the world of fiction – pirates making their victims walk the plank, for instance – this is another story-based concept with no truth behind it.

Wrecking, when the facts are considered, was not practical. Upon seeing lights in an unexpected place, experienced mariners would head in the opposite direction seaward – away from land for safety. Lanterns cannot be seen that clearly when out at sea, unless the crew aboard know, by arrangement, to watch for them. Beacons and bonfires are warning signals, not lures. A law was passed in 1735 making it an offence to create false lights, but this was in connection with signals for the purpose of smuggling, not for wrecking. Whatever the intention of the act, not one person was prosecuted. Master William Pearse of Cornwall was hanged in 1769 at Launceston, charged with stealing from a wreck, but not for wrecking it.

However, tales of salvaging goods from wrecked ships abound, one is of a vicar who had his Sunday service curtailed by someone hurrying into the church to alert the congregation that a ship had foundered on rocks nearby. The vicar promptly begged his flock to remain seated until he could remove his cassock and they could 'start fair'.

In the Caribbean during the sixteenth and seventeenth centuries, ships heading back to Europe from the gold-rich Mexican coast used the Gulf Stream as far as modern-day Cape Canaveral in Florida, then steered for Bermuda to ensure they had the right bearings to cross the Atlantic and to take advantage of the Trade Winds. Not all captains were experienced mariners, and many a ship went down off the Bahamas. But this was error of judgement, poor weather, unsuitable or poorly maintained vessels or pirate attack, not from wrecking.

There is a twist to this danger of the sea. Wrecks did happen because a sailing ship, not easy to manoeuvre in inclement weather, was driven ashore, ran aground or torn apart on jagged rocks. Any wrecked ship was regarded as salvage and cargo washed ashore could be claimed by whoever found it. The professional salvage hunters were called wrackers or wreckers – because they scoured wrecks for what they could gain. But there was never any hint that these unfortunate ships were deliberately destroyed. The term 'wrecker' is therefore true – but not the action associated with it. Among the many court cases involving reference to a wrecked ship there is not one where a captain claims to have been deliberately lured in.

Little Known Fact:
Not until the nineteenth century was it realised that
offering a reward for rescuing people from a wrecked
ship would be a good idea!

There was a nasty side to some of the salvage-hunter wreckers. They regarded what was washed ashore as their property – and woe

Were there really such men as wreckers? (©Erica Guilane-Nachez)

betide anyone who tried to stop their pillaging. This included crew or passengers who had struggled ashore. There is many a report of murder. Except, if these were Spanish ships, heavily laden with treasure and ending up wrecked upon the shores of British-held territory in the Caribbean, then to those salvagers anyone aboard would be classed as an enemy, for until the early-1700s England and Spain were often at war. And enemies of war have never been treated kindly.

Similarly, wrecks happened around the Florida Keys, where there are shallows and coral reefs. A salvage-hunter's delight, but again, no evidence of deliberate wrecking.

However astonishing it may seem, it was not until 1870 that it was realised that to offer rewards for rescuing people from wrecks, before claiming the cargo, would be a good idea.

Contrary to the gruesome tales of luring ships to their doom, is the wreck of the *Postilion* driven ashore on the north coast of Cornwall in November 1732. Local people plundered what was left of the ship and took away everything washed ashore by the tide, but only after every crew member had been brought ashore to safety.

By contrast to the facts, in fiction, wrecking is a favourite sport. It features in, *Jamaica Inn* by Daphne du Maurier and the *Poldark* novels by Winston Graham. For younger readers one of Arthur Ransome's delightful pre-Second World War *Swallows and Amazons* adventure series, *Coot Club*, is set on the Norfolk Broads and features the bird-protection group the *Death or Glories* and their exploits, which include salvaging a wrecked boat. The author of *War Horse*, Michael Morpurgo, wrote the young adult novel set on the Isles of Scilly – *The Wreck Of The Zanzibar*, which was a Whitbread Award winner.

In the movies, there is Cecil B. DeMille's *Reap The Wild Wind* set near Key West, Florida, which gained an Academy Award for its stunning underwater special effects. The opera, *The Wreckers* by Dame Ethel Smyth is set in Cornwall. But alas, the act of wrecking is strictly confined to the pages of fiction or the silver screen. The facts are, deliberate wreckers did not exist and smugglers could be anyone, based in any place, as long as their task was secretive. And profitable.

Chapter Five

Upholding the Law

With authority throughout the Kingdom of Britain, His (or Her) Majesty's revenue men were responsible for collecting customs duty and the enforcement of taxation, in addition to the management and law-keeping of imported and exported goods. Their task today is often thankless and an apparent uphill struggle. Has this always been the case?

What were the various official terms for the Revenue Men?

Coastguard: introduced in 1822 to combat smuggling.

Coast Waiter: a government officer responsible for the shipping and landing of goods conveyed from one port along the British coast to another.

Collector of Customs: chief officer of a port responsible for recording all imports, exports and seizures.

Dragoon: mounted soldiers.

Gauger: revenue officer who measured or 'gauged' the weight and content of barrels or containers.

Landguard: collective name for riding officers.

Landwaiter: customs officer responsible for recording the quantity and quality of imported goods.

Militia: a military force hired as required.

Riding Officer: mounted customs officers first appointed in 1699, specifically to patrol coastal areas.

Searcher: customs officer appointed to issue certificates for imported goods which held a 'drawback' (a refund of duty).

Surveyor: supervising officer of a specified customs district.
Tidewaiter: customs officer responsible for rummaging (searching) ships to ensure that no taxable goods were concealed as contraband.
Waterguard: collective name for customs men at sea.

Little Known Fact:
Dick Whittington was a customs officer before he became Lord Mayor of London!

Originally, the term 'customs' referred to any payments due to the king or the church, and the position comes from 1203 in the reign of King John, younger brother to Richard the Lionheart, when custom payments were made to the State Treasury. From 1275 the *nova custuma* authorised collectors appointed by royal patent, while from 1298, the *custodes custumae* collected customs as tonnage and poundage from various specified ports for the benefit of the Crown. In 1294 the first customs officers had been appointed, names of whom would later include men such as Geoffrey Chaucer and Richard Whittington, better known today as the pantomime Dick Whittington. Chaucer went on to write *The Canterbury Tales*, while Dick became Mayor of London (with or without a cat.)

In the fifteenth century William Lowe, the appointed customs searcher for Dorset, had the huge area of West Dorset, Hampshire and Sussex to patrol, all on his own. Riding his horse in all weathers and through all seasons, he took his responsibilities seriously and was probably the most dedicated customs officer ever recorded. He seized illicit cargo after cargo of contraband wool or leather, culminating in 1452 with a haul of goods funded by fifteen different merchants and destined to be smuggled from England on a Dutch ship. Not surprisingly, Lowe was disliked. In 1453 he was brutally attacked and injured by a disgruntled London wool merchant. Lowe managed to record that he was 'smote with a dagger', which penetrated his nose and plunged into his mouth. Nasty.

January 1643 saw a Board of Customs established, with the very grand title of: *The Ordinance Concerning the Customs for the Continuance of the Ordinance of The subsidy of Tonnage and Poundage*, and the collection of customs became a matter for a Parliamentary Committee. And we all know how pedantic government committees can be!

At sea, there is still a fleet of customs cutters, evolved from these early ideas, used as patrol vessels within United Kingdom territorial waters. They are responsible for inspecting vessels suspected of smuggling drugs, weapons, illegal immigrants, or of exceeding fishing quota regulations. The main difference between modern customs operators and those of the past, leaving out technology, is that today's male and female officers are more dedicated and efficient than their predecessors ever were. Methods of stopping smuggling in the seventeenth and eighteenth centuries were as effective as plugging a leaking water tank with straw. Preventing ships from loading or unloading illicit cargo was nigh-on impossible until the early years of the 1800s when customs officers finally became organised.

It was not always easy to find the men willing to attempt to stop smuggling. In Tudor times, the task of preventing illicit trading in England fell to the 'searchers'. The problem here, however, was that the job could only be acquired via appointment by the Lord Treasurer. Added to that difficulty, the position usually held very low wages with the searcher having to pay for his own deputies and clerks, which he could not do without. The only way to make a reasonable living from what was a thankless job was to accept bribes offered by the smugglers. So not an effective way of policing the Trade. Although for some, it proved a lucrative position even if it was ineffective. Queen Elizabeth I's chief advisor and eventual Lord Treasurer, William Cecil, was offered the post of searcher for Bristol in the 1590s. The wage was £300 per annum – during the late Tudor period typical wages would be nearer to a mere £10 a year. So, not a bad reward for what was little more than blind-eye-turning.

During the early years of the 1700s, the British Government attempted to introduce a Parliamentary Bill to prevent smuggling. The House of Lords voted against the proposal, so that was the end of that. Subsequently, smuggling greatly increased, along with a rise in confidence for the smugglers which, in turn, resulted in a rise of the gangs, and with them, an increase in violence against the men trying to stop them. The smugglers claimed that as the Bill had failed it indicated that the king, and his government of Lords and Commons accepted smuggling because they had no desire to pass an act of law against it. Subtle thinking!

The Bill did, eventually, get passed but it was too late, the South Coast gangs had established themselves and were making their presence heartily known.

Philip Taylor, a Collector of Customs for Dorset from 1716 until the 1720s, wrote:

> The smuggling traders are grown to such a head that they bid defiance to all law and government. They come in gangs of sixty to one hundred men to the shore armed with swords, pistols, blunderbusses, carbines and quarterstaffs; and not only carry off the goods they land in defiance of officers, but beat, knock down and abuse whoever they meet stood in their way.

Little Known Fact:
Even when arrested, smugglers received the sympathy of local magistrates reliant on receiving smuggled goods. On one occasion the magistrate dismissed the charge and ordered the arresting officer to be flogged for his impertinence instead.

It was not surprising that the House of Lords scuppered the Bill. Prior to the 1800s the gentry and merchants enjoying the comforts and luxuries of life, appointed Members of Parliament and Customs Officials, thus making sure that the 'right sort' got the job. The 'right sort', being those who were only interested in a quiet life and had no desire to catch smugglers. As with piracy at the start of the eighteenth century, smuggling was not affecting the pockets of the rich, in fact to many of them smuggling was of great personal benefit; but once industry increased and their businesses began to suffer, minds – and the enforcement of the law – changed.

**Little Known Fact:
Smuggling in England increased after Napoleon was
defeated at Waterloo because there were so many
soldiers and sailors who could not find work.**

The smuggling trade had become an enormous thorn in the British
Government's side after the Duke of Wellington's victory over
Napoleon Bonaparte at Waterloo (18 June 1815). Thousands died
in that battle, but just as many soldiers and sailors returned, a lot of
them wounded and maimed. Even for those uninjured, employment
was difficult to find. For those living near the sea, smuggling was
a salvation. In response, and to be seen to be doing something, the
government created the Coast Blockade in 1818 to patrol the south
coast near Bexhill. Today, we know the Blockade as the Coastguard.

A glimpse at a few Customs House details of smuggling runs:

May: 27 horses with wet goods and 36 horses loaded with tea
June: 60 horses loaded with brandy, 53 loaded with tea
July: 50 horses loaded with tea
Nov: 50 horses loaded with dry goods, 1 cart with wet goods

There were some bold and brave King's Men willing to take the
smugglers on, but they were few and far between, and commanders
were often inexperienced. With little motivation, badly built, slow
vessels, poorly armed and an unwillingness to fight anyway, it was no
wonder that many a smuggler scoffed at the revenue men. Not until
the Napoleonic Wars ended in 1815 and Royal Navy ships and sailors
were freed-up to pursue the temerity of the smugglers did they face
any serious opposition.

Incentives to encourage informers were considered an ideal way to
outwit the smugglers. Except, with most of the magistrates, merchants,
and the smugglers taking advantage of the profits gleaned from the
actual deed, informing carried little to no advantage, particularly
when, if discovered to be an informer, the punishment by the friends

and colleagues of those who had been betrayed would be brutal. The merchants who benefited from smuggling were also magistrates, so there was very little prospect of a sentence, even if someone did give sufficient information leading to a smuggler being arrested and sent to trial. The majority of smugglers were acquitted as a matter of course – assuming an arrest got as far as a trial, which often it did not. A bribe or a word in the right ear would ensure that all charges were, very conveniently, dropped.

Even if the customs officials were good at their job, other tactics went in favour of the smugglers where the letter of the law was concerned. It was not a case of 'bending' the law, but overturning it completely. 'Feigned Prosecution' could be brought to the London Exchequer Courts, with the charge at a later date withdrawn or disproved. This was easy to set up. Aware that a ship and cargo was due in, a local magistrate would send a clerk to pre-arrest a suspected ship in the name of the king or queen, thus ensuring that no one else could seize it or the goods carried, a bit like today: once evidence is in possession of the police, no one is permitted to touch it. When the case reached court the charge would be shown as void because the original 'arrest' was somewhat questionable.

Merchants could also be tipped-off about a possible seizure or search. By the time any customs official came aboard, the cargo was either long gone or skilfully hidden.

Naturally, this nudge-and-wink method was rewarded with a purse of gold or a few contraband bottles of brandy. So good ideas in theory, but of little use in practice.

Once the goods were safely ashore and, so far, the revenue men avoided, the items had to be suitably disguised so that no eager customs inspectors could identify anything as contraband. Tobacco would be packaged into smaller bundles and mixed in with a different legally imported leaf, thus doubling the quantity. Tea, likewise, would be mixed with other ingredients, usually dried rose leaves, which gave a pleasant aroma and added bulk. Spirits would have been brought in as 'over-proof' and had to be 'let down' – diluted with water to achieve double the quantity and a 'drinkable' drink.

The deliveries went either to reputable dealers, merchants who had financed the run, or direct to the many public bars and gin houses. Once with the merchant, and available for sale in a tavern or shop, who would be able to tell where that tot of brandy, glass of gin, several yards of lace or bolts of exquisite fabric had originated from? Certainly not the revenue men.

What did the smugglers call the revenue men?

Bluebottles (interesting that this remains a derogatory term for policemen.)
Gobblers
Preventy Men
Shingle Pickers
Watersharks

Chapter Six

The Gangs

Popular fiction, movies and such, tend to lead us to believe that smuggling was carried out by a few dare-devil, or desperate, fisher-folk. Indeed, in some places, and depending on what, where and how was being smuggled, this is so, but the big money was in the hands of the gangs. Highly organised crime by highly organised leaders, but were these gangs guilty of more than just smuggling?

Smuggling was not restricted to a few men out for a lark after an inebriating tot or two, or three at the local pub, with a sudden off-the-cuff fancy to row across to France, pick up a couple of half-ankers of grog and row back again. Smuggling was a highly organised business, and many of the men were disreputable ruffians who thought nothing of violence and murder to gain that essential profit. One gang member from East Sussex calmly sent a customs official to his death without any hesitation…

As dusk settled, a local militia officer was out on routine patrol along the cliffs of East Sussex near Cuckmere Haven. Expecting a delivered cargo the smugglers hid themselves, but fearing the officer would spot their landing activities some of the gang quickly altered the positioning of the piled lumps of white chalk which acted as easy-to-see cliff-edge markers for the customs night patrols. Darkness descended, and with the essential markers no longer indicating the safe pathway, the poor man tumbled over the edge of the cliff.

The gang members heard their victim's desperate pleas for help and found him hanging on by his fingertips to the cliff edge. One of the gang deliberately placed his boot on the man's clutching hands, callously sending him to his death.

The ideal plot for a 'who-done-it' murder-mystery tale, perhaps?

**Little Known Fact:
Not all smugglers were sailors or had anything to do
with the sea.**

Where smuggling was rife men worked together as 'smuggling companies', some were notorious for their viciousness, others quietly got on with the secretive mission in hand, but these were in the minority. Most of the more unpleasant gangs operated in the south-east of England. Gang members were not always seamen, but landsmen – land-smugglers – who were based near or operated along the roads leading to London in particular, but also to the larger, inland, towns. The seamen brought the cargo in, the gangs collected and dispersed it. If there was trouble, they were ready for it. For the most part, however, a bribe of a keg of brandy or a packet of tobacco was enough to ensure a clear run. But cross the gangs and these rough, tough men could be frightening.

These gangs usually had between forty to fifty men, but for a large haul of contraband, gangs could unite into enormous groups of two or three hundred men. The King's Men, ill-informed, under-manned, under-armed and under-paid rarely had any hope of intervening, let alone stopping such formidable opponents. Two hundred determined smugglers, with their 'bodyguard' wielding stout ash poles (think Robin Hood meeting Little John wielding his quarterstaff) could walk straight through a poorly armed force of ten or twenty young and inexperienced revenue men. While there were rival gangs, who would have had no hesitation in attacking a revenue man or an opposing gang trespassing on each other's designated landing sites, there was also a camaraderie, a brotherhood of sorts, between the Men of the Free Trade. When four smugglers drowned on the French side of the Channel, the French brought the bodies back to England for burial, not remarkable in itself, but at the time, England and France were at war with each other.

Smuggling soon started to hit the coffers of the government, and the wealthy, harder and more frequently. Something had to be done. As with Caribbean piracy earlier in the eighteenth century, when the rich were not affected very little was undertaken to eliminate the nuisance.

Baccy for the clerk… (©Stephen Orsillo)

When commerce and individual pockets began to feel the pinch the response was a different story.

By the late 1780s the government began to see the sense of deploying the military in a more effective way. The customs men became better equipped with better firearms, better boats and more reliable 'intelligence', which meant they stood more chance of seizing contraband.

Even so, the gangs were no pushover. They were armed, rough, tough men and were completely ruthless when ensuring potential informers kept their mouths shut. Betray a gang, and it was likely you would end up dead on a beach with no hope of your murderer being identified, let alone caught and punished. These gangs also had one advantage over the military, government and law. Smugglers and those who supported them were, on the whole, ordinary people: villagers, farmers, servants, poorly paid workers. The sort of people who would not betray anyone involved with the smuggling trade, for the smuggled goods were for their benefit. They knew a bargain when they could get one.

The smugglers were clever, and the gangs were, for a time, very successful. But their dominance was not to last.

Who were the gangs and where were they based?

The Hadleigh Gang

From the Suffolk town of Hadleigh, the 100 men of this gang fought against local dragoons with the intention of recovering a seized cargo. The interesting thing about Hadleigh is that it lies a good forty miles inland. Each man in the gang owned two horses – that is a veritable mounted force far stronger than anything the local authorities could muster. The gang's largest battle with the preventative men was in 1735, when their storage place was found and the customs seized the hidden contraband. They temporarily re-stored it at the George Inn in Hadleigh, but in retaliation more than twenty of the gang turned up to retrieve their property. In the fight which followed, several dragoons were injured and one was killed. The smugglers managed to reclaim their goods but seventeen of them were recognised and subsequently arrested. Immediately after their trial two were hanged. Undeterred, the rest of the gang continued their trade. It was not until twelve years later that the leader, John Harvey, found himself in Newgate gaol before being transported for seven years to the American Colonies. That was still not the end of the gang's activities, for a year later they reclaimed another lot of contraband which had been seized and stored in the King's Warehouse at Ipswich.

The Northover Gang

Hailing from the area around Burton Bradstock in Dorset, the Northover Gang, named for the family of the same name, the father and his sons had an altercation with the coastguard boatmen in December 1822: William Forward and Timothy Tollerway were on patrol. Hearing whistling, which they believed to be smugglers' signals, they spied two boats coming towards the shore and four men on the beach. Creeping along the beach Forward and Tollerway met with the men who dropped the tubs they were carrying and ran off. Tollerway kept an eye on the abandoned contraband, while Forward seized a dozen more tubs after firing his pistol to summon help. Realising he was alone, the remainder of the gang surrounded him. Tollerway ran to give assistance and fighting broke out. The coastguard patrol arrived but most of the gang escaped. Their leader, James Northover Junior, and William Churchill, however, were arrested and sentenced to fourteen months in Dorchester gaol.

Lessons were obviously not learned, for in 1825 James issued a threat to kill the chief coastal boatman from Bridport after a landing had been discovered. Ignoring the threat, the officer and his companions gave chase. Joseph Northover struck the officer rendering him unconscious and the smugglers escaped, but James Northover served time at the gaol twice more, and was impressed into the Royal Navy in 1827 for yet another offence.

The North Kent Gang

This gang worked along the coast from Ramsgate and Reculver to the river Medway, and were based at Burntwick Island, where their local knowledge of the mudflats gave them a distinct advantage over the blockade men.

In 1820 their use of violence was noted: unloading contraband in March of that year, the blockade came across the gang. A fight followed in which one officer was seriously injured, but the gang fled with their cargo. In June there was another affray near Herne Bay. Several of the blockade men were injured after the gang shot at them with pistols and muskets. Returning fire, the blockade wounded two smugglers, who managed to get away –with the cargo. Their next run did not go so well. Two of the gang were arrested, but the gaol where they were imprisoned was set upon by their comrades and they escaped.

During the spring of 1821 forty of the gang gathered at Herne Bay to land a cargo, with twenty more men armed with bats and pistols to protect them. On this occasion, however, the batsmen and tubmen had partaken of too much pre-run 'hospitality' at the nearby Ship Inn and were somewhat the worse for wear. Led by Midshipman Sydenham Snow, the blockade men appeared – drawn by the noise that the drunken smugglers were making.

Fighting broke out and Snow was wounded twice. The smugglers fled with their cargo and Snow was taken to the Ship Inn, where he died the following morning, but he had supplied information about several of the men whom he had recognised. Five of the gang were arrested and sent to London for trial ... but were acquitted on a legal technicality.

The story does not end there. A group of blockade men decided to ambush the gang at Westgate-On-Sea. They seized the cargo, but a midshipman was wounded and the smugglers escaped, but again some of them were recognised. Eighteen men were arrested, four went to the gallows, with the others transported for life to Van Diemen's Land (now known as Tasmania).

The Hooe Gang

Hooe, in East Sussex, is not far from Herstmonceux Castle. The gang used the ruins to hide their contraband and discouraged any interest in the castle, particularly during the hours of darkness, by spreading lurid tales of terrible ghosts haunting the tumbledown walls. James Blackman, the landlord of the Red Lion Public House, was a member of the Groombridge Gang, attached to the Hawkhurst Gang and was also the leader of this lot at Hooe. Beyond those small snippets there

Graveyards and old ruins made a good hiding place for contraband. (©Kolbass)

is, alas, little information, except that those ghostly rumours still exist about the castle even today.

George Ransley's Gang (also known as the Aldington Gang and The Blues).

In the 1820s, Aldington, on Romney Marsh in Sussex, could boast the Ransley Gang. In the churchyard are the graves of two Ransley brothers executed near Maidstone, Kent, for smuggling. Interestingly, the gang would occasionally use that same church and its grounds for hiding their contraband.

Little Known Fact:
One smuggler got so drunk he mistook a blockade man for one of his own gang.

The gang operated small runs prior to 1820, but by this date they had become increasingly daring. On one of their first big runs they brought in tobacco, salt and spirits from Boulogne to Sandgate where over 200 landers and batsmen were waiting to bring the cargo safely ashore. Attempting to stop them, several preventative men were injured. The following year, the blockade patrol discovered the landing party at Camber Sands and violence erupted. Four smugglers and one blockade man were shot dead, and many more on both sides wounded. Two of the gang were captured, although one report tells of the leader, Cephas Quested, being so drunk he mistook a blockade man for a smuggler, handed him a pistol and ordered him to shoot at any officer. The subsequent trial and hangings of the men captured meant that nothing of note happened for a few more years.

George Ransley then became their leader. He came from a farming family, although it seems George turned to smuggling when he had the good fortune of his plough digging up a hidden cache of spirits, which provided him with enough money to buy a grand house at Aldington. Next in command was George's father-in-law, who had a reputation of viciousness – although so did most of the gang.

Ransley was businesslike and efficient with organising the runs; he had solicitors when required and a surgeon on stand-by for any of his wounded men. But his career was to come to an abrupt finish in 1826.

There had been a fight at Dover in July, with a preventative man being killed. Prudently, the gang dispersed, and thought they were safe. They thought wrong. Ransley's house was surrounded in the early hours of one morning by the blockade officers accompanied by a few of London's Bow Street Runners. Ransley himself was caught and committed to Newgate for trial. Seven more of the gang were arrested, with a further eleven captured not long after. Fourteen members were sentenced to hang in January 1827, but were transported for life to Tasmania instead. They were charged with 'more than eighty people assembling armed with firearms.'

George, also sent for transportation, thrived in Tasmania and was buried there in October 1856 with his wife, Elizabeth, buried alongside him in January 1859. He has descendants still living there.

The Hawkhurst Gang
Hawkhurst is a village about ten miles inland from the Kent and East Sussex coast. Between 1735 and 1749 the Hawkhurst Gang terrorised the area and became known as the most notorious and feared gang in all of England. They brought in silk, brandy and tobacco from Rye and Hastings, and up to 500 men could be called upon to work as tubmen and batsmen when needed. One of the first references to the 'Holkhourst Genge' was in 1735, but within five years they were dominating smuggling operations throughout Kent by threatening anyone who went against them – including other smugglers.

Their regular inn was the Oak and Ivy at Hawkhurst itself, where they stored contraband before it was transported to London. With the profits from smuggling, the leaders, Arthur Gray and his brother William, built a large house with its own storeroom to the western edge of the village. The gang also operated in Goudhurst, using the church as a store – where there were tales of a tunnel running from the crypt to the Star and Eagle Inn.

As a gang, they ambushed and attacked customs officers at Robertsbridge, Sussex, in order to reclaim a cargo of tea which had been seized. One gang member, known as 'Trip', found out about the several hundredweight of reclaimed tea being taken under armed guard back to Hastings. Trip organised a retrieval attempt resulting in thirty or so smugglers joining forces. After partaking of some fortificational courage at an alehouse en route, they attacked the tea cargo's guard on the outskirts of Robertsbridge. The fight that followed was successful for the smugglers, not so for the officials: one of the customs officers was killed and several dragoons were captured and offered for ransom.

The gang joined with the Wingham Gang in 1746 in order to bring ashore almost twelve tons of tea (that is a lot of tea!) the Wingham men attempted to leave the landing site earlier than intended and were set upon by their so-called partners. Seven Wingham men were injured, and the Hawkhurst lot made off with several valuable horses which belonged to the Winghams. There is no account of whether the horses were returned, either amicably or by stealth.

Inevitably, law-abiding men, despite the general benefits of smuggling, started to grow fed-up with the gang's increasing acts of tyranny, and led by local militiaman, William Sturt, a villagers' retaliation happened in April 1747 at Goudhurst in Kent. Word was leaked to the gang of this planned rebellion, and confident of their influence and power, marched into the village, not expecting to meet with barricades and a small army of people determined to put a stop to their bullying. The gang had underestimated the bad feeling and suffered a humiliating defeat.

One of the gang, George Kingsmill, was shot dead and he is buried in Goudhurst churchyard. His brother, Thomas, was later arrested and hanged at Tyburn in London, with his body being brought back to Goudhurst to be hung in chains – his body tarred and placed in an iron cage-like structure which was hung from the gallows and left to the mercy of crows, rats and weather.

Another member, William Fairall, was also executed and his body displayed on the gibbet in his home village of Horsemonden. Does his ghost still linger there I wonder? Maybe the ghosts of other gang members wander our coasts, creeks and hidden inlets, ever watchful for the next ship carrying a cargo of contraband to drop anchor ...

Chapter Seven

The Battle of Sidley Green

The aim of the coastal blockade and the revenue men was to put a stop to smuggling, to arrest the smugglers and to confiscate the contraband. Was it as easy as that sounds?

Little Common is a village in East Sussex located near Bexhill-on-Sea and grouped around the crossroads on the main road from Hastings to Pevensey.

George Gillham (1773–1831) led the Little Common Gang, although like many another smuggler, he used a nickname so that he would not be identified by the revenue. Fortunate for us, we know his real name and some of the other gang members' nom des plumes: George Gillham went under the name 'Smack', Thomas Gillham was 'Peckham' and Thomas Shoesmith was known as 'Boathook'.

According to George's tally books, which can be seen in Bexhill Museum, he paid additional smuggling helpers ten shillings a night, whereas a farm labourer was lucky to get less than that for an entire week's work.

Cellars beneath his cottage, which is still standing, were used to hide contraband, as did his workshop opposite. That all sounds most benign, but it is likely that the gang was responsible for the murder of blockade man, William Welch. In 1824, his body was found on Bexhill beach following strong rumours that he had taken bribes in order to ignore the smuggling runs. It seems he double-crossed them, for he was waiting with a group of fellow blockaders to seize their vessel as it came in. The lugger hastily put back out to sea, but the enraged crew captured Welch. He was beaten, tossed overboard and left to drown. Or so the lurid tale goes.

Gillham also, presumably intentionally, directly insulted the king. The gang concealed their two luggers the *Longboat* and the *Princess Charlotte* near the Star Inn Bridge. The surrounding marsh was difficult for the authorities to patrol and accurate local knowledge was needed to cross it safely, particularly at night. It is somewhat amusing that Master Gillham had named the *Princess Charlotte* after George III's daughter, Charlotte, the Princess Royal (1766–1828). An eighteenth century way of a smuggler thumbing his nose at a king and his laws?

In February 1822 a large number of smugglers had gathered outside the Star Inn, expecting the arrival of the *Princess Charlotte*. Before she made landfall the blockaders arrived, heavily armed, and set about breaking up the assembled men and one of the smugglers was shot dead. Then, in 1828, another fight occurred at Sidley Green to the north of Bexhill....

Friday night, 3 January, smugglers were unloading a lugger drawn up as close as possible into the shallows, and tubmen were taking their kegs up the beach to disappear into the night. Then, a shout from the Bexhill end of the beach. A signal shot fired ... another! The blockade!

Batsmen hurried into position forming stout lines each side of the landers and tubmen, their 6ft long ash-poles hefted in readiness of defence. A race against time and King George IV's men, then began – the cargo had to be taken away before enough blockade reinforcements from the Galley Hill Martello Tower arrived.

Relying on the strength of the batsmen the landers and tubmen continued about their work. The batsmen surrounded the small group of blockade men, shots were fired, but in the dark and confusion no one knew who had fallen, or from which side.

Now unloaded, the remaining tubmen and landers moved as fast as they could up the beach, clutching their precious contraband. The lugger put out back to sea, with her captain intent to meet at the Bell Inn next evening to collect his payment. Some of the smugglers left with the lugger, the rest, their job finished, hurried off into the darkness, but one of them was a traitor and informed that the gang would head for a favourite hiding place 2½ miles away at Sidley Green. Unaware of the betrayal, the smugglers hurried up the Sea Road, a dirt track linking what is now Bexhill Old Town to the beach.

Hoping to head them off, the blockade men rushed through the narrow, cobbled lanes of Bexhill Village shouting for assistance. Extra reinforcements from the Martello Tower ran to join them. With forty well-armed men there was hope of catching the smugglers red-handed. Fights started, rousing the villagers who leant out of their windows to shout where the blockade men were – warnings that anyone who did not remain quiet would be shot were ignored, for the villagers were on the side of the smugglers.

A cart had been taken to the Bell Hotel Inn and willing helpers unloaded the brandy it carried and quickly hid the kegs in the cellars along with a wounded smuggler. The cart was emptied and hurriedly removed, all lamps and candles were doused, and with barely a moment to spare the blockade men dashed into view – but the inn was in darkness and they ran on past.

By now, most of the tobacco and alcohol was on its way to London, or the tubmen were striding away across the Sussex Downs, but the fighting continued and involved eighteen batsmen, still wielding their ash-poles, and the same number of landsmen – against forty blockade men armed with swords, cutlasses, pistols, muskets and bayonets.

The leader of the blockade fell, but his men stood firm and the smugglers were, inch by inch, driven back. At Sidley Green the fight reached its climax. Quartermaster Collins had his head cleaved open by a batsman; smuggler Timothy Smithurst was shot through the neck, his body found the next day with his hands clasped firmly around the shaft of his ash-pole – or what was left of it.

Deaths and injuries occurred on both sides, but not one smuggler was captured alive, and all the contraband, save for a few tubs that had been dropped on the beach, was delivered to its various destinations.

The story does not end there!

The men of the blockade were determined to track down the scattered gang, and arrests were made after a local girl of 'loose character' (a prostitute) gave information that led to ten men being arrested. One of them was Charles Hills, her lover, but he turned informer in exchange for a lesser sentence. Had he spurned her in some way? Did she take revenge to punish him for a transgression against her? Whatever the reason, be warned: if you are going to take up smuggling, keep your girlfriend sweet!

Chapter Eight

Naming Names

Some Individual Smugglers

The most infamous of the Essex smugglers was Mr William Blyth, (1753–1830). He was Pagelsham's churchwarden and greengrocer, and had the delightful nickname of 'Hard Apple'. Stories about him range from the fact that he would wrap the fruit and vegetables he sold in pages from the Parish Register, that he would drink his fill in the Punch Bowl pub, then eat the glasses, or when a bull unexpectedly interrupted a game of cricket on the village green, he grabbed the bull by the tail and used his cudgel to scare it off. He could outsmart the revenue as well. Once, when his vessel, laden with contraband, was boarded the cargo was seized and removed to the revenue cutter. Not making a fuss, Blyth calmly sat down to sample what was in the kegs with the uninvited guests and got them all drunk. When the revenue were dead to the world, he retrieved his property and left the men sound asleep on the shore. In 1786 two ladies, wishing to return to England, from Dunkirk were transported by Blyth and his crew, with the women chaperoned by John Harriott, who knowing about the smuggling runs, had intentionally set out to find Blyth for this very purpose. The twist to the tale is that Harriott was a magistrate.

Many of the Blyth family are buried in Paglesham's churchyard. It is also somewhat ironic that one of William's sons went on to work with the Thames River Police.

Gabriel Tomkins

About eight miles south of Tunbridge Wells in western Kent, Gabriel Tomkins led the Mayfield Gang, which flourished in the first half of the eighteenth century, landing their contraband along the Sussex coast at Hastings and Eastbourne. When two of the gang were captured at Dungeness and taken to the gaol at Lydd, the Mayfields attacked the prison in order to set their comrades free, although Tomkins suffered a minor wound during the raid. Another time, a warrant for arrest was put out for Tomkins's brother on a charge of tying up an officer on Seaford Beach – the modern equivalent would be 'assaulting a police officer.'

Tomkins was arrested again in 1721, bribed the gaoler and escaped, but was recaptured and taken for trial in London, where he was sentenced to transportation (to the American Colonies, Australia had not yet been discovered). However, he turned King's Evidence, gave the authorities a lot of valuable information and was consequently set free. He did not 'go straight' though, for he was arrested again three years later and then again in 1729. Giving evidence about corruption within the customs office, he was awarded the position of Riding Officer and rose to an even higher rank within six years. Poacher turned gamekeeper indeed.

His duty to king and country did not last. In 1746, as a highwayman, he robbed the Chester Mail and in 1747 joined the notorious Hawkhurst Gang. Soon after, he was recognised and arrested for the mail robbery and was hanged in 1750.

The Colonel of Bridport

The Bridport free traders operated from Seatown to Charmouth in Dorset, under the leadership of 'The Colonel' and used the church tower at St Gabriel's Mouth as a hiding place for contraband. One cargo was nearly intercepted by revenue men and had to be hastily hidden by sinking it in the sea, but it floated free and came ashore near Eype Mouth, not far from West Bay – to the great delight of the locals who 'liberated' it. Apart from this mishap, the Colonel's gang was highly successful. They were never caught, and regularly supplied the taverns at Bridport and the nearby area.

The brothers William and Emberson Dowsett, according to the Maldon Customs House, were frequently involved in skirmishes regarding the suspected carrying of illicit cargo, although their smuggling days came to an abrupt end when William's boat, *Neptune*, was chased by the revenue in 1778, and ran aground. Dowsett and his crew had to abandon ship in the shallows and make a run for it. When the revenue seized the vessel and boarded, they found over 390 half-ankers of spirits along with 8cwt of tea and 3cwt of coffee. Three weeks later, the same revenue men captured Master Dowsett, and thus ended his career.

Little Known Fact:
Joss Snelling was in his nineties – and still smuggling.
He was also presented to Queen Victoria!

As with elsewhere, Kent smuggling started with the wool trade, but the Trade increased, and the first gangs were formed by the Huguenots who fled France towards the end of the seventeenth century. One such gang was the Broadstairs Callis Court Gang, led by Joss Snelling who continued smuggling (allegedly) well into his 90s. He and his gang have their lasting reputation from a battle fought with riding officers in the spring of 1769. Eighteen smugglers lost their lives or were arrested, although Joss and four others managed to flee to safety. One riding officer was wounded and taken to the Captain Digby Inn which, as in most cases like this, temporarily became a hospital. Joss, however, lived to smuggle another day, and was even presented to Queen Victoria as the 'famous Broadstairs smuggler'.

Jack Rattenbury

There are several notorious men on the Dorset coast roll call of smugglers, although fisherman Jack Rattenbury could also count as a Devonshire man as he came from Beer, on the Devon side of Lyme Bay. The son of Anne Newton from Beer, and John Rattenbury from nearby Honiton, Jack was born in 1778 and worked for over thirty years as a Lyme Bay fisherman, seaman and pilot, but wrote about his other life as a smuggler in his *Memoirs of a Smuggler*, published in 1837.

Rattenbury spent some years as a privateer and sailed as far as New York and Newfoundland. His smuggling days led him to the Channel

Isles and Cherbourg, bringing his contraband back to several places along the south and west coasts and the Isle of Wight. For his fishing (and smuggling) trips he sailed in a lugger called *Brothers*, which had been built in Beer in 1807, and was owned by a Master Abraham Mutter, a shipwright from Burton Bradstock. Seized in 1808 with over 100 small casks of liquor aboard, *Brothers* was sentenced to be condemned for illegal trading, and broken up in 1809.

By 1814 Rattenbury was finding the 'trade' to be almost at a standstill, although the occasional 'fishing trip' was a diversion from total boredom. Writing his memoirs probably kept the hankering for adventure at bay.

In turn, Sir Walter Besant wrote a novel in 1896, *'Twas in Trafalgar Bay*, about Rattenbury's exploits. Rattenbury's own *Memoirs of a Smuggler* gave his readers a fascinating insight into the world of nineteenth-century smuggling, but the crafty so-and-so mentioned no names, gave no condemning information, nor included any of the secretive tricks of the trade. While interesting, his narrative frustratingly leaves out the exciting detail, but certainly immortalises the author.

Thomas Benson

One of North Devon's more notorious gentleman; a merchant trader, general scallywag and a smuggler, I could not resist using this interesting man in my nautical adventure series. Although his exploits as a smuggler were later than my *Sea Witch Voyages*, set in the early 1700s, Thomas Benson would have been a young boy when my fictional ex-pirate came to drop anchor in the North Devon harbour of Appledore. The young Thomas, therefore, made an ideal character for me to include.

Appledore, situated on the North Devon coast, is a quaint town rambling up a steep hillside with narrow, cobbled streets, secretive alleyways known as 'opes' and an interesting history. Viking raiders attacked here, there may well have been a second battle between the English and the Normans shortly after 1066 – much of the surrounding land belonged to defeated King Harold II or his family, and the area saw action during the English Civil War. Squatting beside the estuary confluence of the rivers Taw and Torridge, Appledore was – and still is – the gateway to Barnstaple several miles up the river Taw, and to Bideford, up-river along the river Torridge. Bideford, then, was one of the major import towns in England for tobacco. Sadly trade was to diminish as the river silted up.

Thomas's father was Squire John Benson, a respected shipbuilder and merchant trader living at Knapp House, a Jacobean residence that had a frontage to the river Torridge. The house is still there today, although modernised and altered. After the death of his two elder brothers, Thomas inherited the family business in 1743. He legitimately transported large quantities of tobacco from the Virginian Colonies and was a highly successful trader, exporting woollen goods made locally, and he owned a fleet of fishing vessels which sailed to the cod banks of Newfoundland. He also smuggled contraband.

When England went to war with Spain (again) and France joined the fracas in 1744, Thomas took advantage of the situation by refitting one of his vessels as a man-o-war and used it as a privateer – legal piracy – and thereby achieved additional financial reward.

In 1747, he entered politics when he was elected, unopposed, as a Whig Member of Parliament for Barnstaple, and was subsequently awarded the title High Sheriff of Devon, an office which he held until 1749. The honour was most welcome because he could now obtain government contracts, which included transporting convicts as indentured slaves to Maryland and Virginia, therefore subsidising the outward journeys of his regular tobacco trading runs. Things did not always go so well, however.

In 1750 he had an argument with customs authorities, owing them a large sum for unpaid import duty of tobacco. Thomas had quietly built up an illegal business of smuggling, tax evasion and insurance fraud, all of which were to lead to his undoing. He operated many of these secretive schemes via Lundy, a rugged island offshore from the North Devon coast in the waters approaching the Bristol Channel. There is a local saying about Lundy: if you cannot see it from the mainland, it is raining. If you can see it, it is about to rain.

Leasing the island at a rent of £60 per annum, he devised a plan to smuggle in his tobacco and avoid paying import tax. Lundy was ideal for smuggling. Offload the cargo, conceal it, then sail into Appledore harbour with the rest of the cargo that did not carry such a high import duty. When conditions were right, quietly smuggle the Lundy merchandise in to be sold secretively. Added to this, instead of transporting some of the unfortunate convicts to the Americas, he took a few of them no further than Lundy where they remained in bondage to work on his smuggling scams, but he kept the fees for shipping them to the colonies.

By 1752 Benson was increasingly under pressure from the customs authorities. He instructed his lawyers to pursue every loophole to postpone eventual judgement, but the total debt to the Crown amounted to £8,229, a substantial sum of not much less than £800,000 in today's money.

Financial ruin was imminent, so Benson devised an insurance fraud using the oldest vessel in his fleet, *Nightingale*. He insured both ship and cargo of pewter and linen, then chose trustworthy Captain Lancey to assist in the ruse. The plan was to deliberately scuttle the *Nightingale* and claim the insurance value. At first, Lancey would have none of it, but eventually he yielded, lured by the promise of financial reward.

Nightingale dropped anchor in the Lundy Road to shelter from a (conveniently) strengthening westerly wind. Her entire cargo, apart from 350 bushels of salt, were offloaded and concealed on the island and then, slightly offshore, the ship was sunk. The crew were rescued by a passing boat – with the wrecking well timed for a vessel to be nearby.

Unluckily for Benson, the truth soon came out. Captain Lancey was arrested, tried in February 1754 and hanged for fraud on 17 June of the same year at Execution Dock in Wapping, the usual place for death sentences passed by the Admiralty Court. Benson fled to Portugal where he had several contacts, abandoning Lancey to his fate, and he died in the 1770s after building up another successful trading company in Lisbon. Whether it was a legitimate one we do not know – but his life was certainly the stuff of a plot for a good nautical adventure.

Were there any women smugglers?

Certainly women helped unload and carried contraband – the 'domestic' goods such as fabrics, tea, lace and such – to a safe destination. Lace, silk, even ropes of tobacco, could be wound around the legs and body and safely hidden beneath the voluminous layers of skirt and petticoats. A long, full, skirt was an ideal hiding place for bladders filled with alcohol, and the women did not risk being searched for the revenue men were forbidden to accost any female, or take the liberty of peering beneath her outer garments.

The *Hampshire Chronicle* of March 1799 commented:

A woman of the name of Maclane, residing at Gosport, accustomed to supply the crew of Queen Charlotte with slops went out in a wherry to Spithead, when a sudden squall coming on, the boat sank; the watermen were drowned, but the life of the woman was providentially saved, by being buoyed up with a quantity of bladders, which had been secreted round her for the purpose of smuggling liquor into the ship.

In the publication *Old Folkstone Smugglers*, which contains a collection of seafaring anecdotes, there is a story of the Three Mackerel tavern frequented by revenue officers, but the dispersal of contraband managed to continue beneath their noses. According to one of the stories, two bold young women entered the tavern disguised as laundresses carrying between them a large basket of lady's 'intimate' clothing – petticoats, stockings and chemises, items strictly out-of-bounds to male prying fingers and eyes. Needless to say, concealed underneath was more than fresh-laundered garments!

Beyond assisting on land, however, there is no evidence for women serving aboard any smuggler's vessel, but lack of evidence does not mean they were not there. Women did serve aboard Royal Navy and Merchant shipping – disguised as young men. We know of two pirates because they were captured and had their story made public: Anne Bonney and Mary Read sailed with Calico Jack Rackham in the early

1720s and were arrested with him and his crew. The men hanged, Bonney and Read 'pleaded their bellies' (were pregnant) and had their executions postponed. Mary died of gaol fever before she gave birth, as for Anne... no one knows what happened to her.

Little Known Fact:
There were probably a lot more women, disguised as
men, than we think serving aboard Royal Navy Ships!

A handful of women, who for various reasons abandoned their life at sea, made their past career known, but how many kept quiet and served as crew dressed as men remains unanswerable. One clue to suggest that there were more women aboard Royal Navy ships than we think can be found in sea-shanties. Surprisingly, there are several songs about women who are found out. If this was a rare occurrence, why the shanties?

Disguise for a woman posing as a man was relatively easy. Few people bothered to wash either themselves or their clothes, so garments were rarely removed. Breeches and shirts were loose and baggy, making female curves simple to conceal. Many a woman could pass herself off as a young lad with no reason to shave. Some women would fashion pipes to disguise how they urinated. Many men carried venereal diseases and bled in the nether regions, plus, menstruation would have been irregular – if at all – because of poor nutrition. The hardest part for any female would be to mimic male mannerisms: drinking, belching, farting. But then, I doubt it was the 'ladylike' women who went to sea.

Women ran various trades during wars. They had to, men were away fighting, many did not come back. Life, commerce and trade had to continue. Women managed the shops and taverns, kept the accounts. It was no different for the eighteenth century than during the two world wars when women worked in munitions, engineering, on farms or driving ambulances and buses. It is inconceivable that women did not play their part where smuggling was concerned. How many were the brains and organisers behind a run? They must have been good at their job because not one of them was caught.

HOW?

Chapter Nine

Ponies Trotting through the Dark?

A Smuggler's Song by Rudyard Kipling

IF you wake at midnight, and hear a horse's feet,
Don't go drawing back the blind, or looking in the street.
Them that ask no questions isn't told a lie.
Watch the wall my darling while the Gentlemen go by.

Five and twenty ponies, trotting in the dark,
Brandy for the parson, 'baccy for the clerk.
Laces for a lady; letters for a spy,
Watch the wall my darling while the Gentlemen go by!

Running round the woodlump if you chance to find
Little barrels, roped and tarred, all full of brandy-wine,
Don't you shout to come and look, nor use 'em for your play.
Put the brishwood back again – and they'll be gone next day!

If you see the stable-door setting open wide,
If you see a tired horse lying down inside;
If your mother mends a coat cut about and tore,
If the lining's wet and warm – don't you ask no more!

If you meet King George's men, dressed in blue and red,
You be careful what you say, and mindful what is said.
If they call you 'pretty maid,' and chuck you 'neath the chin,
Don't you tell where no one is, nor yet where no one's been!

Knocks and footsteps round the house – whistles after dark –
You've no call for running out till the house-dogs bark.
Trusty's here, and Pincher's here, and see how dumb they lie
They don't fret to follow when the Gentlemen go by!

If you do as you've been told, likely there's a chance,
You'll be give a dainty doll, all the way from France,
With a cap of Valenciennes, and a velvet hood –
A present from the Gentlemen, along o' being good!

Five and twenty ponies, trotting through the dark,
Brandy for the parson, 'baccy for the clerk.
Them that asks no questions isn't told a lie –
Watch the wall my darling while the Gentlemen go by!

Copyright permission courtesy United Artists, London

The Gentlemen. (©Jackin)

'Baccy:	tobacco.
Brishwood:	brushwood.
Laces:	French lace, or silk threads for tying stays.
Woodlump:	a woodpile.
Valenciennes:	French lace from the town of the same name.

Born in India in 1865, Joseph Rudyard Kipling was an English journalist, storyteller and poet. He died in 1936, but his evocative tales and poems of India and soldiering still stir the souls of his readers. One of his books, *Puck of Pook's Hill* was published in 1906 and is a collection of short stories set in varying periods of English history. Narrated by two children and an elf, Puck – 'the oldest old thing in England', there are elements of accurate history entwined with magical fantasy.

One of the items included is *A Smuggler's Song*. Written as if a smuggler is issuing a warning to curious children. The poem beautifully conjures the atmosphere and detail of a clandestine smuggling run, while the repetitive style of the chorus highlights the emphasis of 'don't be nosey while the smugglers go about their business'. But, how accurate is its meaning? Is this delightful poem nothing more than a romantic ideal? How did the smugglers go about their smuggling …?

An essential part of smuggling was the organisation and timing. It would not be wise to take potluck, sail in on the next most convenient tide and hope there would be a few men waiting around to help unload. Small items could be hidden by one person – lace, or a package of valuable spices for example: you went on board, sailed across the Channel and, whistling innocently, disembarked at Dover or wherever. Not exactly easy to do this with brandy barrels! Tide, time of day, men to bring the cargo ashore and distribute it required coordination and planning. Everything hinged on the arrival of the boat. What was rarely fixed to precision was the landing site.

The revenue patrols had to be outwitted, care had to be taken to ensure there was no unintentional mention of the rendezvous. To counter the 'inconvenience' of patrols, smugglers made arrangements for optional landing sites at various locations along the destination coast. As soon as the contraband boat appeared out at sea the men awaiting its arrival could quickly ensure that no militiamen were in the vicinity, signal to the ship and head for a suitable cove or beach. Ships could sail much quicker than men on foot could march or ride on horseback, so at any sign of danger the smugglers would signal a change of plan and use the next cove along or the other side of a wide estuary. By the time customs officials had hurried to the spot where the contraband had been unloaded there would not be a trace of the activity remaining, except for a few scuffed footprints.

The duty of the smuggler's 'spotsman', with his superb night vision, was to guide the ship into a safe anchorage. He would be a local man born and bred, who knew every creek, river, bay, beach, nook, cranny and tidal current along his designated stretch of coast. With the coast clear – yes, this phrase does come from the days of smuggling – he would signal the ship waiting out at sea and bring her in.

Smugglers' vessels were occasionally painted black or dark colours, and had dark sails. The romantic idea of a cargo being brought in by the light of a full, bright moon is just that – romantic. Most smuggling runs occurred when there was no moon or a thin sliver. Our reliance on street and electric lighting has dimmed our night sight, but it is amazing how well things can be seen at night when the eye is used to the dark.

To signal, the spotsman would show a light of some sort, but not a bright lantern or flaring torch. On clear nights a tinderbox spark could be sufficient, but a more usual signal was the flash of an unloaded pistol. Flintlock pistols were fired by pouring gunpowder into the priming pan and pulling the hammer back; squeezing the trigger releases the hammer and creates a spark, which in turn causes a flash and the resulting explosion would send the lead ball down the barrel. To charge the pan and fire without 'bullets', or even the barrel attached, can give a distinctive blue flash. The term 'flash-in-the-pan' relates to the process where the flash occurs but no lead ball is fired.

Lanterns were used where it was safe to do so – where no one land-based could see the glow. High, seaward-facing windows were built into the eaves of houses along the coasts or cliff tops; a candle or lantern could be set here at the right hour, and only the crew of a ship would see it. Similarly, a light shown from within a cave was only visible to the waiting boat. Some lanterns had shutters that could be rotated, giving the appearance of a flashing light, others had only one seaward facing glass un-shuttered, or there was a spout lantern which projected a single beam of light enhanced by a round piece of bullseye glass. Beacons were not used to signal a vessel to come in, but for the opposite reason – to warn of danger. To set light to a furze beacon was an instant warning that the shore was unsafe. It was illegal, of course, to light such warnings, but by the time the revenue men had arrived at a heaped pile of burning furze the smugglers were long gone.

Little Known Fact:
Coachmen coming from Dover to London would pass on secret messages to the smugglers using their trumpets.

Messages about cargo and landing places were passed in secret by ingenious methods. One, used especially in Kent, was via the coachmen travelling between Dover and Canterbury or London. Blowing particular notes on a long horn or trumpet would alert the tollbooths and inns ahead that a coach was approaching. All coaches had their own tunes or series of notes to be quickly identified, so it was simple for the coachman to add in different tunes that had different meanings known only to a select few.

How many songs can you think of that would be suitable for smuggling? *Candle In The Wind* perhaps? *Secret Love*? *Diamonds Are Forever*…?

Anything up to 200 or so men could be hidden in the dunes, scrub, or beneath the cliffs, waiting patiently for a boat to appear offshore. A sloping beach and a small vessel, shallow on the draft, could be run up on to the beach or shingle, with the cargo tossed ashore or passed to the waiting men. Bigger ships had to ride the tide at anchor or with sails aback (set at angles to hold the boat still – a little like holding the handbrake on in a car). Cargo would be transferred to smaller boats to

Waiting for the signal to come ashore. (©Fenatka)

bring ashore. Depending on the tide, the tubmen had to wade in and out of the surf, or a chain of men would need to be formed.

For flat-bottomed vessels, and in isolated coves where the tide fell back a long way, it was a more straightforward matter of dropping anchor, wait for the tide to ebb, then walk out on to the sand or take carts out to the boat. One eye had to be kept on the turn of the tide though, for in some places the incoming water moved pretty fast. This sort of operation was easy to conceal from prying eyes, for the carts, or ponies and mules, would be out on the beach at low tide anyway, collecting kelp (seaweed) or cockles, muscles, whelks and crabs.

If there were cliffs, the tubmen had to carry their loads up steep wooden ladders or haul it up on ropes. And all the while watch would be kept for the revenue men, with well-armed batsmen standing guard in case of trouble. Once unloaded the ship would make sail as soon as possible, given the vagaries of wind and tide. On land the goods would be quickly and efficiently carried off to a designated hiding place or intended destination. Away from the beach and immediate area it was difficult, if not impossible, to prove that contraband had been brought ashore. Catching the smugglers in the act was the objective. Before the 1800s it was rarely achieved.

During daylight, signals had to be suitable, and secretive. A canvas sail or linen bedsheet was hauled across a cliff-edge cottage roof or hayrick to act as a marker. Everyday things could be a signal for a landing: laundry spread on bushes, a cart waiting at a certain point, cattle grazing in a specific field, a flag hoisted atop a church steeple, a small upturned boat on the beach, fishing nets spread to dry on the rocks ... any pre-arranged signal could indicate that it was safe to be 'put on the spot' (another common phrase from the smugglers). The landsmen would appear as if from thin air and take over, under direct orders from the lander, the man with the brains in charge of the operation. He it was who organised the landing party – the brawn – needed to carry the cargo ashore, along with the tubmen, ponies, or carts required to transport it. Speed, efficiency and down-to-the-last-detail organisation was essential.

The men on land were as important as the seafarers. The landing party, and the transporters, were shadowy figures flitting through the morning mist or waning moonlight. The brawn were labourers, farmworkers and such, men – and women – desperate to add a few shillings to their low wages. Apart from a very rare handout from the Parish Relief, there was no social benefit for the poor in the eighteenth century, even if they were close to starvation. Indeed, many of the gentry and new rich – the merchants rising to the echelons of the upper class – despised the poor. To the wealthy, these wretches brought poverty upon themselves through laziness, drunkenness and slovenly behaviour. No matter that the harvest had failed, the expected shoals of sprats or herring had not arrived, or that the Land Acts of Enclosures had taken away the fields for growing food and grazing livestock. The benevolent caring for tenants by characters in fiction, such as those in ITV's *Downton Abbey* drama series is, sadly, misleading. Assisting the smugglers, in whatever capacity, was, for many a struggling family, the difference between staying alive or dying.

A man took what work he could find in order to scrape a living for himself and his family, even if that meant risking his life or freedom. A few hours working as a landsman or tubman could earn enough to keep his family alive for a month or more.

Financing the acquisition of the contraband was the first, most important problem to solve. Most smuggled goods were paid for on delivery, so funding had to be found. Early on, in the years when money was not so easily available (no credit cards back then!), payment was through barter: bales of English wool swapped for kegs of French wine or bundles of lace. As smuggling, and the list of contraband items expanded, while exported items declined and imports (and taxes) increased, arrangements for more suitable financing began to change also.

The commonest form of financing came via groups of land-smugglers joining together as a syndicate. Located along the highways and thoroughfares from the coasts to London and the larger towns, with between them plenty of capital to invest and the expectation of a high profit in return, it was a lucrative way to make money. In the West Country, there was the early equivalent of 'crowdfunding', where everyone in the village and nearby area contributed a share of the outlay, depending on what they could afford per run – an outlay of anything from a few shillings to several pounds. The advantage of this was that no individual lost everything, or could be held responsible if anything went wrong. Additionally, the risk of being 'shopped' by an informer was slight as few people knew who else was involved.

Kent and Sussex was slightly different in that smugglers had good access to London and the Home Counties where there was more wealth. Small groups of rich individuals were more likely to put up the money, or individual merchants would fund a potential run or two. A publican who owned his own tavern could stock his cellar more cheaply via the smugglers, or a draper could acquire silks, brocades, velvets and lace for a more reasonable outlay. Financiers in the latter half of the eighteenth century possibly paid entirely for larger runs taking only the profit, not the cargo, as a reward. There is only speculation for this, as no evidence can be produced because nothing was ever written down. And no one in this lucrative enterprise was ever caught doing it.

Rich French brandy and Dutch gin distillers would finance their own supplies. They organised the details of the runs, and used their own boats which would drop anchor off the English coast at a prearranged place. Alcohol smuggling for the distillers and brewers was very big business. Avoiding importation duty ensured good profit and low outlay.

A shopping trip ... for firkins and kilderkins

You have your money, collected from people clubbing together or a rich patron. Now you need someone to go shopping. A trustworthy traveller willing to cross the English Channel to France, Spain, or wherever. Or maybe you can trust the master of a ship to get what you need. Or perhaps you have an agent who lives abroad. The details have been made and confirmed with a shaken hand, either the way we shake hands now, but with the addition of spitting on your palm first, or there is some evidence that what we call a 'high five' was an old way of sealing a gentleman's agreement.

The cargo is stacked, ready and waiting on a quay or wharf to be loaded. The tide turns, the vessel comes into harbour and is moored alongside or drops anchor. This will be a legitimate vessel, everything, so far, above board, unless there is export duty to pay. In which case all this will also be done secretly in a quiet backwater cove away from prying eyes.

Several continental harbours in the mid-to-late eighteenth century gleaned vast profits from their share of supplying smuggled items in high demand in Britain. Not surprisingly, the main ports were the same convenient cross-channel destinations in use today: Boulogne,

Calais, Cherbourg, Dieppe, Dunkirk, Le Havre and Flushing in the Netherlands, now known as Vlissingen. Holland was a significant supplier of many goods suitable for smuggling, but especially for Dutch gin.

To counter the plethora of English Smuggling Acts, the French used the small Breton harbour of Roscoff as a depot for supplying contraband, particularly to Devon and Cornwall. Prior to 1767 Roscoff had been nothing more than a fishing hamlet. It soon expanded into a town where merchants gathered to 'do business'. The French were happy to encourage smugglers because they, and their agents, were the lavish spenders of the day. One record shows that 230,000 livres of tea – that is nearly 110 tons – was purchased and smuggled from Nantes in 1766. The French authorities were aware of what was going on. Goods were openly transferred from large barrels, bales, casks and containers into smaller, more manageable 'packaging' before being loaded aboard that waiting ship.

A hogshead barrel was the usual, standard, wooden container, holding up to 140 gallons of liquid, but these required winching

Brandy for the parson. (©Nctfalls)

aboard, or offloading, so smaller kegs would have been more usual for the ease and quickness of smuggling. Smuggled tobacco and tea came in small parcels, easy for one man to lift and carry. These would be securely wrapped in tarred or oiled canvas or leather pouches in order to keep the contents dry, particularly during landing when they could be dropped in the surf. Waterproof packets and kegs tossed overboard would stay afloat for hours, ready to be collected later at a more convenient moment.

Alcohol went into smaller half-anker barrels called 'tubs' (hence the tubmen who carried them away from the landing site). These barrels each held about four gallons, were especially made for ease of carrying and to rest snug against the body. Off the tubman would stride into the quiet of the night, covering many miles before dawn broke. If ponies were used, the tubs fitted neatly across their backs. Acquiring the contraband was relatively easy. Getting it ashore and distributed was the hard part.

So what are firkins and kilderkins?

$4\frac{1}{2}$ gallons = 1 pin
1 pin = $\frac{1}{2}$ firkin
2 firkins = 1 kilderkin
2 kilderkins = 1 barrel
1 barrel = 36 gallons
6 barrels = 1 tun
$\frac{1}{4}$ tun or 54 gallons = 1 hogshead
$\frac{1}{2}$ tun = 1 butt

You can now boast that you know your firkins from your kilderkins!

You've found a financier, you have purchased your boatload of contraband and safely brought it across the Channel. Now you have to, as quickly and furtively as possible, get it ashore and away... but what if there was trouble ahead? On the whole the gangs helped each other, but not always. Greed got in the way of being 'a gentleman'.

There were battles, but not just between smugglers and the revenue men; rival gangs could cause as much trouble if they felt an interloper gang was intruding on their patch of territory. The threat of danger mostly came from the revenue men, but it was as dangerous for them – to apprehend a gang of rough and desperate smugglers took courage. No smuggler would follow the etiquette of gentlemanly swordplay if there was a fight. They would make use of head, hands, shoulders, elbows, knees, feet … in short, every dirty trick they could think of – and more beside!

Flintlock pistols and muskets were ideal for short range, but limited to one shot and not very accurate, and these were weapons for the king's men or the gang leaders, few fishermen or farm labourers could afford a firearm. Anything that came to hand served as a weapon: hoes, shovels, pitchforks, clubs – everyday tools that could be snatched up quickly.

No weapons available in a hurry? A revenue man unexpectedly appearing along the coastal path on patrol? A finger poked into an eye could be effective, or a boot scraped down a shin, an elbow jabbed into the stomach, or a knee rammed into the groin could incapacitate an opponent. And the best weapon? Run!

Chapter Ten

The Tricks of the Trade
(or how to fool the revenue men)

Smugglers had a number of tricks up their sleeves (or in their boots, or for women, under their skirts) to fool many a customs officer. A common belief is that if a boat was in danger of being spotted by the revenue, the cargo would be tossed overboard and lost forever. That seems something of a waste. Is it true?

A barrel of illicit brandy could look like any other normal barrel. Inserting a rod into the bunghole would reveal a full-depth amount of cider or ale, but hidden compartments were secreted at the top and bottom where packets of tobacco could be stored. Or the barrel itself was actually two barrels, one cleverly built within the other where brandy could be hidden. The hollow heels of shoes and boots could carry small items. Boxes of tea or tobacco could easily be fitted between the timbers of a ship, neatly made to look like the wooden planking of the deck, or small packets could be strapped beneath the flared trousers worn by many a sailor, or sewn within the lining of a coat. Hats could conceal small cotton bags fitted into the crown, or beneath a lady's skirts, or even as padded 'thigh bags' on a gentleman.

Most boats carried wooden or canvas fenders – bag-like structures suspended over the sides in order to protect the hull from being damaged against a wall or quay when moored. These fenders could be hollow with the space inside used as storage.

Little Known Fact:
Contraband tobacco was hidden from prying eyes by twisting it together to make it look like rope.

All these tactics were simple, and initially eluded the revenue men, but with more experience and thoroughness being gained, more extraordinary concealment lengths had to be thought up. Disguise was one adequate ruse. Tobacco could be bound up to look like rope from thin cord to thick hawsers. Coiled on deck or stored in a locker alongside real rope it would be overlooked.

If transporting contraband to its eventual destination was not an immediate possibility, then suitable hiding places had to be arranged.

The favourite hiding place for storing contraband in fiction is usually a cave, but for practicality, apart from a few remote caves in Devon, Cornwall and Wales, these are often not the best choice. A lack of dry conditions and access being the main detriment. A cave might be easy to get to from the landing beach at low tide, but high tide, although concealing the entrance from unwanted snoopers, could make everything wet and salt-contaminated, and for several hours a day limited opportunity to move the illicit stores. And what is easily accessed by the smugglers at low tide could be as easily approached by

Was this cave, located near Stackpole, in Pembrokeshire, Wales, used by smugglers? (©Tony Smith)

the revenue. Some caves, however, where they suited their purpose, were used. Samson's Bay Caves in Devon being one such known storage place.

Church crypts were ideal, ready-made hiding places, used because of the taboo of disturbing the dead, but the resident parson had to be a staunch customer or suitably distracted at the right moments. Smugglers, it seems, did not have the same reluctance about meeting ghosts or coming across the remains of skeletons. Digging a shallow cache was common, using local knowledge of the sand dunes. With a decent hole excavated and the opening well hidden, smuggled goods could be left until the all-clear came. The quickest way to hide your contraband if unwanted company appeared was to secrete it in the most convenient place. The sea. Shove your tubs in a weighted sack tied to a length of rope to a heavy bag of shingle, join another length of rope to the other end with a bunch of feathers and an inflated pig's bladder attached, then toss it into the shallows. It would stay there until you came back for it. There were risks: the marker 'flag' could come adrift, or the weight become untethered, or more frequently if the barrels were poorly made, seawater could leak in and ruin the alcohol within.

Over time, this crude method of concealment became more sophisticated. Barrels could be lashed together and weighted so the make-shift raft floated below the surface, this 'sown crop' as it was known, would be collected later, or floated to a safer rendezvous point. Or maybe the current would take the secured barrels upriver on an incoming tide, right under the noses of the revenue men.

The use of secret tunnels are something of a myth. Their locations gleefully divulged to present-day tourists after several drinks at old 'Smuggler's Rest' pubs situated within a mile or so from any point along the coast. It is odd that nearly all of these illusive entrances to secret tunnels are conveniently lost or bricked up....

Digging tunnels would have been a major accomplishment, and unlikely to have been kept secret – we are talking eighteenth century here. Where tunnels do exist they were intended as storm drains or natural occurrences, as they are at Porthcothan, Cornwall. There are a few tunnels that may have legitimate origins built for smuggling purposes, but they are few and far between.

There were other ways to fool the revenue, several of them quite amusing. One tale is of a group of passengers and crew coming ashore distraught that the captain had died on the voyage. The revenue summoned the local doctor who went aboard with the coffin-maker. Before long, a solemn procession made its way across the harbour and through the town to the church, stopping at the inn to give the dead captain a fitting send-off – with the accompanying revenue men well 'attended-to'. The slightly less dignified procession set off again, the coffin now aboard a cart which soon left those walking behind. The vicar was there at the church to receive the coffin. Quickly it was emptied of what it actually contained – contraband – before being filled with sand, resealed and buried with due solemnity.

What about those ponies trotting through the dark? As many as 100 men or more could be involved with the transportation of the landed contraband, and twice as many horses. There are several tales about smugglers and their four-legged assistants. Kipling's 'five-and-twenty ponies' is accurate; hooves were bound with rags, or left unshod – especially the hard-hoofed, sure-footed native ponies, such as the Exmoor and Dartmoor breeds of Devon. Nose to tail, headcollar rope tied to the tail of the pony in front, making their way at a sharp, steady pace through the lanes or across the moors…. The men oiled and greased the ponies' coats to make it hard for them to be grabbed. Another ruse: many a smuggling horse-owner would teach his equine friend to 'whoa' or 'giddy-up' in reverse order. If a carter was commanded to stop, he would willingly shout out 'Whoa!' and off the horse would canter, away up the road. Much to the bewilderment of the revenue man.

Then there were the horses who knew their way home. Stories tell of smugglers being ambushed or stopped on the road, their animals laden with contraband. The horses would quickly be set loose and whipped off out into the darkness, the men would fight or talk their way out of trouble, or simply run and hide, but with the evidence galloped away what charge could the smugglers be arrested on? Come morning, there would be the horses, waiting by their own field or farm gate, burden intact.

Exmoor ponies were ideal for carrying contraband and 'trotting through the dark'. This is the author's own Exmoor pony: Mr Mischief. (©Kathy Hollick Blee)

Nor is that a fanciful tale, horses know their way home very well. Brewery drays, milkmen and bread deliverymen, in the days of horse and cart and regular rounds, would find their horses stopping automatically at the next house on the route. My own four ponies, solid and intelligent Exmoors, know their way up the lane to the village pub. I'll not mention how they learnt it!

Workhorses would be 'borrowed' as required. In the morning – as in Kipling's poem – a tired horse would be inside with a bottle or keg of brandy hidden beneath the hay as payment. Not everyone was willing to lend their horses. These were working animals, not pets; by day they had to earn their keep, and a tired or lame horse was no use to its owner. Farmers who begrudged a helping hand (or hoof) were targeted for revenge; their hayricks burned, or returning late from town they might not see the length of rope stretched, at neck height, across the lane.

Betray a smuggler and you might get more than you bargained for. The cunning of our 'gentlemen' expanded as the revenue became stronger and wiser, but on the whole, it was the smugglers who won the day, even if it meant having to toss a cargo overboard in an emergency. But rarely was it done lightly, and always with the intention of coming back to collect it as soon as possible. Although the 'possible' was sometimes later than hoped for.

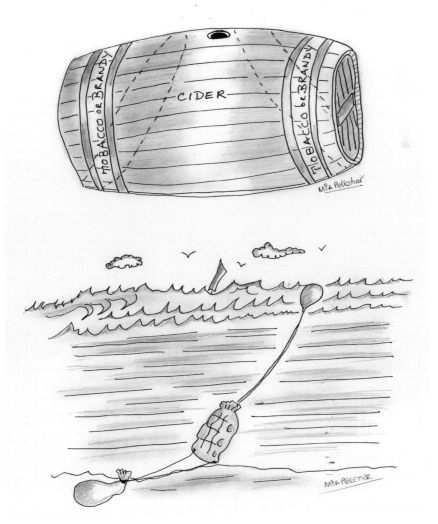

Above, secret compartments in barrels could conceal brandy, gin or tobacco
Below, 'sowing or seeding a crop': contraband could be easily hidden at the bottom
of a shallow stretch of water with the aid of some rope, stout sacks, a heavy weight,
a pig or sheep's bladder, and feathers to use as a floating marker. © Mia Pelletier

WHAT?

Chapter Eleven

From 'Baccy to Brandy

W hat? Anything that held a high import or export tax duty, and illicitly sold at a profit was worth smuggling, but some items seem strange to us now. Tea, tobacco and brandy we know about; but salt? Really?

**Little Known Fact:
The term 'fleeced' (to be cheated) comes from the
wool trade.**

Mercantile goods have always gained or lost their smuggling value depending on demand. Thomas Jefferson, in his pre-presidential days as an American ministerial representative in Paris from 1785, had been involved in smuggling by bringing rice, hidden in his pockets, out of Italy. This was a crime carrying the death penalty. To us it seems odd to smuggle rice, but it was once a rare and valuable commodity.

Silkworms, too, were smuggled from the Far East, as was tea. Spices were exotic and expensive: cinnamon, nutmeg, saffron, cloves – even tulips, which originated from Iran, Central Asia and Turkey, but thrived in the Netherlands from circa 1594 – all were smuggled from where they grew in abundance to where they were prized.

Cornishmen smuggled tin, and needles which could be easily hidden. Jewellery was also easy to smuggle. Gems could be sewn into coat linings or women's petticoats, which were also suitable places to conceal silk stockings and lace. No revenue man would search a lady's undergarments, no matter how high his suspicion that she carried more than 'natural' padding. Precious stones could be prised from their settings and slipped into pockets or even swallowed to reappear and be disposed of at the smuggler's convenience – excuse the pun!

The conclusion of the Napoleonic Wars reignited the English appetite for French goods. Brandy, French cognac and other comestibles were always popular, but stylish people who, in one way or another, had amassed wealth to spend also desired homes furnished in the French manner, consequently the demand for French furniture and art had never been greater. Some trade was entirely legal, but many goods were not, which is where the smugglers came into their own. The trade in risqué French art, both genuine and fake, with some more pornographic than merely suggestive, were sought after and would equate with today's 'under-the-counter' material acquired via covert means.

The importance of wool for England and its economy is reflected even today in British Government. Since the fourteenth century the presiding officer of the House of Lords has traditionally sat on a seat stuffed with English wool known as the Woolsack.

In early Medieval times, English wool was sought after in Europe, especially wool from the Welsh Marches, the West Country and Lincolnshire – the latter two being suitable smuggling areas as trade was primarily with the Low Countries and France. It is estimated that England exported 25,000 bales of wool in 1280, rising to a peak of 45,000 per year, then falling in 1355 to 33,000. That is a lot of wool, a lot of sheep and a nice amount of revenue for the king.

At times of famine, severe weather conditions or disease the wool trade could be drastically affected. The less wool available the higher the demand and the price of fleeces. The term 'fleeced' comes from the wool trade, meaning to be tricked with something that looks better quality than it really is.

Towards the end of the 1200s, without the supply of exported English wool, the industrial areas of Europe were on the brink of economic ruin. To finance his English economy, Edward I negotiated an agreement of a permanent tax duty with the wool merchants, although illicit trading did not become illegal until Edward III became king. In 1337 Edward declared himself the rightful heir to the French throne, which was, naturally, contested by the French and thus began what was to become known as the Hundred Years' War.

By the mid-1500s, English wool exports were beginning to decline, partly because farming increased the meat and dairy production as the population expanded, and partly because the Iberian Peninsula started producing finer wool from high-quality Merino sheep.

In 1566, anyone caught smuggling wool was punished by the left hand being amputated and nailed to a church door as a warning to others. Obviously to little effect as wool smuggling continued apace.

Little Known Fact:
In the seventeenth century about 500,000 pounds weight
of wool was smuggled every year across the English
Channel from Romney Marsh on the south coast.

In the Tudor era, the father of a young lad dabbled in wool smuggling. John was a relatively well-off merchant, but he fell upon hard times after being fined for illegally trading wool. Who knows, had he not been impoverished, his son – William Shakespeare – might have grown up with a completely different lifestyle, not entered into acting and playwriting, and we would have been left far less rich regarding our literature today.

What have cows and hares to do with contraband?

During the Napoleonic Wars, Bonaparte paid people to smuggle gold from England into France in order to support the French currency. The method used was to row across the Channel from Deal, Dover or Folkestone in 'Guinea Boats', although we are not talking small rowing boats here, but huge 40ft long vessels which could take a substantial cargo of gold on each voyage. With twenty-four oars, twelve aside, the men of Kent could cross to France in less than five hours, given the right conditions. On one occasion such a boat overtook a steam-driven vessel and beat it to France. Trying to catch one was a waste of time, best summed up as, 'sending a cow to snare a hare'. Eventually, using these boats became illegal, although that meant little to the smugglers.

Brandy, gin, wine – alcohol in general was the most popular contraband to smuggle. To be economical for space and for ease of storage and carrying, spirits were usually supplied 'neat' or 'over-proof', in the condition that the alcohol came out of the still in which it had been fermented. Dilution would be made prior to sale, or by the purchaser if a merchant or landlord had specifically funded that particular run. Dilution would not be done until the substance reached its destination. No tubman or carter wanted to carry the unnecessary weight of added water. Over-proof spirit that had not been watered-down could be lethal if consumed in quantity, as sometimes happened when kegs were washed ashore after being dumped in order to escape seizure by the revenue men. A tub of abandoned brandy washed up on the beach would be broken open and eagerly consumed. Often with fatal consequences.

The only setback for the consumer at the end of the line, was that in London especially, the water used came from polluted wells, so some rather unsavoury additions such as human sewage, animal excrement and contamination from drowned rats, cats, dogs (and the occasional human baby) were mixed in. Upset stomachs after a visit to the pub were frequent.

In the 1780 booklet, *Advice to the Unwary*, as we have already seen, the author complained that smuggling had a bad effect on legitimate trade in silk, but he also condemned the smuggling of gin. Gin was an enormous problem during the 1700s as it was readily available and cheap to buy because so much of it was smuggled into the country. The author states: 'Great numbers of people sell it by retail without licences, who entice servants, and the lower sort, to drunkenness and debauchery.'

Tobacco was as addictive – and potentially lethal – in the seventeenth and eighteenth centuries as it is today. The 'obnoxious weed' comes a close second as a 'dangerous' substance, but is high on the list of 'best things to smuggle'. Growing it was not easy, for tobacco plants poison the soil, yet in Virginia in particular it was so highly valued that cured (dried) tobacco was used instead of currency. Everyone grew it, from the vast plantation estates to humble Virginian vicars growing a few

Nicotiana plants in a tub on his veranda. Once an importation tax was slapped on tobacco, in came the smugglers.

Much of the smuggling was an ingenious 'scam'. Tobacco from Maryland or Virginia was imported legally into Britain, the duty paid, then exported again with a legal 'drawback' refund paid on import duty. The exact same tobacco would then find its way back into England to be bulked out and increased in quantity by adding ground leaves, herbs, straw and dust, then repackaged and resold. The government's treasury lost money twofold. Questionable tactics, but clever.

There were some very odd things smuggled. Cannons from the iron foundry at Ashburnham, East Sussex, England, were discovered on French and Dutch ships taken as Prizes by the Royal Navy during the Seven Years' War, which ran between 1756 to 1763. The Weald of Kent and Sussex was a major area for the source of iron for London manufacturers in the late sixteenth and early seventeenth centuries. From 1650 the Weald's production became more focused on local foundries for casting cannons. With the war ended, however, the forges fell into decline. The last one to close was at Ashburnham. You cannot help but wonder that part of the downfall was due to smuggling activities – and how on earth did they manage to move heavy things like a ship's cannon in secret?

Little Known Fact:
Lace was once among the most highly prized contraband to smuggle.

Lace was an excellent textile to smuggle because it was lightweight and easily hidden. Lace was being crafted in England, but foreign-made, in particular Brussels and Blonde lace, was highly sought after.

'Blonde Lace' was not an exclusive fashion accessory for fair-haired ladies! Made in the eighteenth and nineteenth centuries in France, this pretty bobbin lace was crafted from silk, with the 'blonde' referring to the natural colour of the thread, not for the wearer's hair colour. Generally, the pattern consisted of flowers and was similar to the finer Chantilly Lace. However, Blonde Lace had a soft texture and suited

An engraving of an eighteenth-century lace maker. (©acrogame)

trimmings that would lie next to the skin, collars and cuffs, for instance. Favoured by royalty, Blonde Lace is depicted in a detailed portrait of Princess Charlotte of Wales (1796–1817) the daughter of King George IV (formerly the Prince Regent) and Caroline of Brunswick. The princess died in childbirth aged only 21.

Brussels Lace was altogether different; a delicate lace made from fine-spun linen which, in order to ensure the thread did not become brittle, was always spun in a damp and darkened environment with only a single ray of light permitted.

First produced in the fifteenth century, Brussels Lace is listed among presents given in 1543 to Princess Mary Tudor, daughter of Henry VIII and Katherine of Aragon. A royal lace indeed!

In order to protect the making of English lace, the import of foreign lace was prohibited by Parliament in 1662. Regrettably, English lace merchants were unable to emulate the quality, so smuggled lace remained in demand. The import ban was lifted in 1699 but Brussels Lace continued to be a firm favourite of Queen Anne.

Kipling's 'Valenciennes Lace' is a bobbin lace originating from Valenciennes in France. The height of its popularity was between 1700 and 1780. Made by hand, it was woven in one piece with the net-like background, the *réseau* fashioned at the same time as the main pattern, the *toilé*. The early lace was made from flax, but there was very little of this hand-crafted lace being made by the time the 1900s arrived because machine-lace had taken over. Another beautiful item superseded by man-made material.

What came first, the teacup or the teapot?

It may seem strange, especially for us Brits with our love of the 'cuppa', that tea was once a valued and rare commodity. For us here in the twenty-first century – be it served in the best china cup or a novelty mug, as strong as 'builder's tea', almost anaemic, (milk first or last?) or with lemon instead of milk, the cup of tea is an established way of life. Few of us English tea-drinkers stray from the dominating brands on sale in the supermarkets, and then there are the varieties of breakfast teas, afternoon teas, herbal teas … loose leaf teas, tea bags … (a choice of square, round or pyramid shaped, a bleached or unbleached bag).

All teas, no matter what flavour, variety or fad, are served by infusing the tealeaves in boiling water and leaving them to brew. The leaves come from an evergreen shrub, *Camellia Sinensis*. Originating in

China as a medicinal infusion, the leaves were pounded into a powder, boiling water was added and the concoction stirred with a bamboo brush. Tea in China became a popular drink during the Tang Dynasty (seventh to ninth century), which was a period regarded as the pinnacle of Chinese culture. But strangely, the tea*cup* came before the tea*pot*.

Portuguese merchants smuggled tea into Europe in the late 1500s, with the fashion for its distinctive taste spreading to England in the 1600s, reportedly introduced by Portuguese-born Catherine of Braganza when she married King Charles II in 1662. It was known in Portugal as *chá* – used today in Britain as a slang term for tea, or as Cockney rhyming slang puts it: Rosie Lea – Tea.

With the establishment of the East India Company, and its Dutch equivalent, the *Vereenigde Oost-Indische Compagnie*, or V.O.C., tea became an even more popular drink, with the Dutch spreading the trade back to the Netherlands and then to the New World. Samuel Pepys encountered tea in 1660 at a London coffee house, but the drink was not widely consumed until the eighteenth century because it was extremely expensive. The price began to fall when Indian Tea, introduced to break the Chinese stranglehold, became widely grown on the Indian continent and therefore easier and cheaper to harvest, transport and import. The luxury beverage became the 'household necessity' that it is now during the nineteenth century, black tea, with milk and sugar added, overtaking green tea in popularity towards the end of the 1700s.

As with all expensive goods that were in demand, were transportable by sea, easy to smuggle and carried a profit, tea was one of the top commodities to be prized by the Gentlemen of the Free Trade. It was estimated by the British Government that three million pounds in weight of tea, every year, was smuggled into England between 1700 and 1750. It is no wonder that the English are known as a nation of tea drinkers. One of the reasons behind the government putting more men, effort and money into ending the smuggling trade was the influence of the East India Company shareholders. Smuggling was publicly condemned in a series of widespread newssheets as being detrimental to the economy as a whole, and was therefore responsible for high unemployment and low wages. Of course, the East India Company did not mention anything about their tumbling annual profits.

Particularly during the years of war and disagreement of one kind or another, the French East India Company played a huge part in the smuggling of tea into England, for annual tea auctions were held in Brittany during the autumn months. Bought at a reasonable price, transported to England and sold for a higher value, but less than that of officially imported leaf, the profits for the French were most rewarding.

Tea gradually became more available as shipping increased in number and efficiency, and it became cheaper to buy. Eventually, the British Government revoked the import tax, and the smuggling of tea withered away as unprofitable by the start of the 1800s. Prior to this, a most unpopular Tea Act of 1773 provoked a certain Tea Party in Massachusetts, but we will explore that topic later.

Salt was an essential, not a luxury, but that meant everybody needed to buy it. Before refrigeration, salt was needed for preserving food, but believe it or not, salt has been one of the most taxed commodities throughout history dating back to ancient times. During the late 1600s, William of Orange needed money (yet again to finance war). In 1693 he brought some of his Dutch accountants from Holland who advised a higher import duty on tobacco, spirits – and salt. Although in this case, the tax was added to the manufacture, not the sale, but still affected the cost of buying it. George III followed his predecessor's example, and raised the rate again in 1767 to assist funding the cost of the American War of Independence. Not until 1825 was the tax lifted.

For the fishing industry, French sea salt was the best for packing and preserving fish, but from 1803 until the 1815 English victory at Waterloo, rock salt from Cheshire had to suffice. The drawback was that this type of salt stained the fish and lowered its value. Salt was also required for cheese making, another staple diet for many a poor family.

Romper Lowe, from Allostock in Cheshire, led a gang of salt smugglers. He was quite good at it, and the local cheese makers appreciated his efforts. To distract the revenue men he and his sidekick, Lach Dennis, would bide their time at the local public house giving the impression that they were about to head off on a salt–smuggling run. Meanwhile his gang was quietly doing the deed.

Lowe's smuggled salt was hidden in the chapel, while coffins made of 'seasoned' oak held a different type of seasoning. The parishioners knew perfectly well that the salt was there, for at times, although covered with sacking, the heap would be in full view.

One night, William Carter, the tithe collector, parish constable and devout church-goer, was awoken by Lowe's gang making more noise than they should when their cart, laden with salt, became stuck in a ditch. Constable Carter did his duty and sent his servant to assist in pulling the cart out.

WHERE?

Chapter Twelve

Quiet Cove to Sandy Beach

The West Country: Cornwall, Devon, Somerset, Dorset

Smuggling, by necessity in the days before the aeroplane, was confined to coastal regions and rivers. As road systems improved and much of the population moved from farming or fishing communities to the ever-expanding towns, so transporting smuggled goods increased.

Nor was smuggling exclusive to England, Ireland, Scotland and Wales. There were smugglers in France, Spain, Holland, Italy ... the Americas. Everywhere in fact, but is our popular idea of smuggling relevant to different areas, was it a case of 'one method of smuggling fits all?' Were smugglers the same from Lands' End to John O'Groats, from Cardigan Bay to Scarborough?

The nature of smuggling in the West Country was entirely different to the peak period of smuggling in Kent, Sussex and Essex in the eighteenth and nineteenth centuries. There, gangs of men operated; in the West Country, it was of a much smaller scale, which included the size of the cargoes landed. The gangs operated protected by men armed to the teeth with cudgels and pistols, the Cornishmen relied on stealth and made use of brain not brawn.

The Cornish towns of Boscastle, Polperro and Trebarwith, along with the rugged cliffs and caves near Tintagel, were among the most efficiently used landing sites frequented by smugglers. In the Elizabethan period, the Killigrew family, who established Falmouth, raised their money, status and influence direct from smuggling and piracy. This was possibly endorsed, albeit quietly, by Queen Elizabeth I herself; in public however, especially when a Spanish ship was involved,

A West Country lane – such hidden highways were used for safely transporting illicit cargo. (©Tony Smith)

she reprimanded the Killigrews. The Spanish Armada subsequently put an end to any diplomacy with Spain.

Cornwall was the first landfall spotted by East Indiamen returning from the far east; in 1763 several such vessels avoided paying import tax by offloaded £20,000 of silk, china, tea and other goods offshore of Falmouth harbour – that is over £3 million in today's money!

There were several famous Cornish smuggling families, one of the main contenders being the Carters of Prussia Cove. The cove itself is said to have been named by John, the eldest son, who admired Frederick the Great, King of Prussia. John himself retired from smuggling in the 1800s.

Black Joan and her brother, Fyn, operated near Looe Island, with Joan supposedly having murdered a black man whose ghost still haunts the island. The Trelawneys had owned the island from the early 1600s and a series of their tenants were reputably efficient smugglers through the eighteenth and nineteenth centuries.

Another smuggler, Tristam Davey, was being pursued by a revenue boat. Knowing the coast as well as he did, he headed for a reef of slate rock and cleared it, but the men chasing him had no idea of the hidden danger. Their boat hit the surf-covered rocks and Tristam shot the captain but left the rest of the revenue crew to drown. Their ghosts haunt the cove to this day...

Dutchman, Hans Breton, who lived in Cornwall, smuggled only one keg of brandy, but it lasted him more than twenty years because he was partners with the Devil. Or so legend says.

Pepper Cove, a few miles north of Porthcothan, was so named for the huge amount of pepper brought ashore there when spices were heavily taxed. North of Hayle there were quite a few landing points: Hell's Mouth and Ralph's Cupboard – a smuggler immortalised by its name, being among the many. Then there is St Ives Bay, where the tax collector was one John Knill, who also turned his hand to smuggling, even while in the office of mayor during 1767, and Roger Wearne, a customs officer allegedly helped himself to contraband.

The church at Lelant stored contraband, which would then find its way to the nearby kiddlewink – a Cornish term for a small pub. Sennan's inn was owned by a farmer who, with the assistance of the landlady, Anne George, ran an efficient smuggling trade. She fell out with him, however, and testified against him. Later, in 1805, she appeared in court as witness against another smuggling prosecution, but she was regarded as such a spiteful gossip that the magistrate dismissed the case.

Padstow and Penzance have their share of smuggling stories, as does Truro, Mousehole, Helston and Mullion Cove – in fact it would probably be easier to name the very few places along the Cornish coast that were not involved in smuggling! But were they 'gentlemen', these West Country men of the Trade? Probably not.

Thomas Benson of Appledore has already been mentioned, but he was not the only Devonian to smuggle contraband. George Pulman, in *The Book of the Axe* (the river Axe, not the wood chopper) said of Beer, in Devon, just around the corner from Dorset: 'When the coastguard was inefficient and the exciseman lax, the Beer men were the very kings of smugglers.'

With much of the contraband coming in via the Channel Islands, the Beer, Branscombe and Seaton fishermen were so skilled at the Trade that in 1750 dragoons were called in to assist the revenue men. A unique style of lugger, built at Beer, were between 25–35ft in length and were manned by four crew, although not every vessel was designated for smuggling, but those that were only used for fishing were few and far between.

On one occasion, furious villagers from Branscombe, Sidbury and Salcombe Regis, marched in protest carrying an effigy of the local toll-keeper which they then burned. His crime? He informed on the smugglers. For over a century a succession of vicars at Salcombe Regis were the brains behind the runs, holding their planning meetings in the vicarage and using the church as a hiding place for the goods brought in. There are supposed to be tunnels leading from the church to the vicarage.

As with Cornwall, the Devon coasts and moors, the narrow, hidden lanes and the remote villages combined to make Devon a smugglers' heaven.

Little Known Fact:
Cornwall is a peninsular with one, long, continuous coastline, while Devon is the only English County to have two completely *separate* (and very different!) coasts – North Devon and South Devon.

North Devon's coastline is far more rugged than that of the south, and tended to play host to the smuggling trade during the more favourable weather and tides of summer. Compared to South Devon the coves and beaches to the north are not so welcoming, with their rocky shores and dangerous currents, in addition to the strong winds that come direct across the Atlantic – real sou'westers. It took a good seaman to steer a vessel safely to shore along the north coast. Even coming into the confluence of the Taw and Torridge rivers, bound for Barnstaple or

Bideford, held its dangers for a hidden sandbar covered by turbulent surf had to be negotiated before Appledore or Instow harbours could be reached. The one big advantage: the revenue men kept a closer eye on Cornwall and the South Coast. With the isolated miles of Exmoor nudging right against the sea, seafarers who knew the coast between Ilfracombe and Porlock found that smuggling contraband was relatively risk free – discounting the mood of tide and weather, that is. Once landed and hauled up the cliffs contraband could be taken openly across Exmoor, using the sturdy native Exmoor ponies. The remote moors, the winding lanes and the many miles of rugged coast – Devon was a smuggler's paradise, but a revenue man's nightmare.

After London, Bristol was the second most important port in England from late Medieval and early Tudor, to relatively recent times.

Little Known Fact:
In Bristol, several of the important eighteenth century buildings, still in use today, were built funded by money made from smuggling.

Prior to the eighteenth-century money-making business of the slave trade and accompanying cotton and tobacco industry, which brought wealth to merchants, many of Bristol's businessmen financed their income through smuggling. In 1545 John Smythe part-financed the building of his Ashton Court estate, now owned by Bristol City Council, from the profits of smuggling. Smythe was one of the elite Bristol merchants who was involved with about five per cent of Bristol's contraband, not merely including the goods themselves, but with favourably influencing customs officials. When a man was offered wine to the value of over £300 on an interest-free credit that man is hardly likely to search the ships of his generous patron. If he did, the debt would quickly be called in.

Bristol Grammar School, founded in 1532, was also partly funded by smuggling, while Corn Street's eighteenth century exchange building was the place where merchants conducted their various business transactions, although it is in the surviving ledgers that the evidence for smuggling comes to the fore. The discrepancies between what these merchants made, and what they actually declared, is quite startlingly different!

The Somerset coast saw its share of smuggling, with the secluded villages being less complicated, on occasion, to land a cargo than within the bustle of Bristol. At Weston, for instance, there was no easy-access road, only a track which had the grand title of the 'Bristol Road'. The sand dunes were well suited for smuggling, although there were not many locals living there during the 1700s, beyond a scatter of farmers and fishermen. There was little opportunity to sell what was harvested from the land or the sea, for the markets were few and far between and Bristol was a trip of several hours away. Beyond Weston, there was Minehead, Porlock, Watchet and Bridgwater, themselves all smugglers' havens. At Bridgwater the revenue officers, at one time, admitted to being fully aware of wine, brandy and over 2,000 packages of Irish Linen smuggled in over a course of three days, while at Watchet most of the vessels in the harbour were used for smuggling contraband.

Watchet was a particular thorn in King Charles II's side. He ordered his Surveyor-General of Customs to inspect the town and the immediate area and to particularly look into the increasing smuggling problem. The resulting report states:

> The whole town has grown exceeding rich and now have as great an overseas trade as Minehead.... At Watchet it was found that several small vessels had no other business but that of running goods, and that the collector of customs there usually sat drinking with the masters of ships while gangs of men were unloading them.

The Collector was William Dashwood, who preferred sitting in the Blue Anchor or the Ship's Tavern rather than be about his official duties. His assistant, Mr Perry, snitched on his master to the Surveyor-General. In consequence, Dashwood was suspended and the informer appointed in his stead. I doubt that Mr Perry was very popular with the taverns' landlords or the townsfolk.

Little Known Fact:
One Dorset smuggler taunted the revenue men by
dropping his breeches and mooning at them!

Despite the difficulty of heavy seas and bad weather, Chesil Beach, Dorset, is an ideal smuggler's landing site. It has an almost unique formation of a shingle bank stretching from Portland to Burton Bradstock – about seventeen miles. Smugglers judged where they were on moonless nights by the size of the pebbles: larger at Portland, smaller at the other end. Contraband was carried across the shingle and sunk in the quiet Fleet Lagoon behind, left there to be collected later when the coast was clear. Wrecks were common. In 1762 a Cornish ship ran aground and the crew drowned, with the cargo drifting towards Portland. The customs officers hoped to seize the contraband part of the cargo, but the locals were as determined to claim it for themselves. In the end, the revenue had twenty-six tubs and the locals ten. Another storm in 1822 caused a similar rivalry battle when tubs of alcohol secured to a raft went adrift. Taking to their boats, the revenue went after it, as did the smugglers. The revenue thought they had won, but the smugglers surged ahead and claimed the goods. As they sailed victoriously past the revenue men, the smuggler's helmsman loosened his breeches and slapped his bare buttocks. Nice to know that smugglers had a sense of humour … and maybe smugglers preferred moonless nights because they did their own 'mooning'!

In November 1720, when government efficiency was very poor, fishermen near Burton Bradstock found twenty-three ankers of brandy and two barrels of wine which had been 'sown' (hidden in the sea). The contraband was stored with the Excise Officer at Abbotsbury, a Master Whitteridge, but was re-seized by William Bradford, the Lord of the Manor's bailiff, who claimed that his master should have the haul for his own use. The customs officer attempted to retrieve the contraband but was obstructed by local men. Finally, he called in the army. Arriving at Abbotsbury on 16 November, a Dorchester regiment of horse faced the townsfolk gathered to oppose them, but Bradford changed his mind and surrendered the contraband. A while later, the Lord of the Manor complained to the Secretary of War about the use of mounted troops, and claimed that the goods were his as the brandy and wine was salvaged from a wreck. The matter was even discussed in Parliament – but dismissed. There does not seem to be a record of who finally kept the booze.

The Dove Inn in the Dorset town of Burton Bradstock was a known contraband store. Situated across the bay opposite Lyme Regis, Burton Bradstock was one of the main landing places for smugglers of the western part of the south coast. It was here, and at another landing place at Swyre a little further along the Jurassic Coast, that the Northover Gang operated. West Bay and Bridport, too, saw their share of these smugglers exploits.

In October 1719, during the course of one week, Dorset played host to two impressive runs. One was at Worbarrow Bay, along the Purbeck Coast, with the second near West Bay and Bridport. Five ships were involved at Worbarrow, while the Bridport venture brought in a huge quantity of brandy and salt – in full view of the customs officials who were unable to do anything to stop the run.

While brandy was the main item smuggled into Dorset, the usual haul of tea was among the highest commodity, but coffee and salt were also listed as seized goods, along with pepper, cocoa, vinegar and paper.

For the Lyme Custom House, in addition to Burton Bradstock, Bridport and Abbotsbury, their attention was centred on Beer, just across the border into Devon. Many local families were involved with smuggling – families known to us through the records, such as the Bartletts, Farwells, Orchards and Oxenburys.

In the 1800s, after the cessation of the Napoleonic Wars, the Kent and Sussex coasts were strengthened against smuggling by establishing the Coast Blockade in 1817. Dorset, however, was not covered by this new government scheme but in 1822, because of the enormous rise in smuggling, there was a further rethinking of the preventative service. The waterguard, revenue cutters and riding officers, were all brought beneath the jurisdiction of the Board of Customs, with a new title being given: the Coastguard. To house these men, cottages were built at suitable points along the Dorset coast.

The old customs lookout above Chesil Beach, Dorset. (©Becky Stares)

The new coastguards were not necessarily effective though. General instructions to the Coastguard included:

> All officers and Persons employed in the Coast Guard, are to bear in mind that the sole object of their appointment is the Protection of the Revenue: and that their utmost endeavours are therefore to be used to prevent the landing of uncustomed goods, and to seize all persons, vessels, boats, cattle, and carriages, in any way employed in Smuggling and all goods liable to be forfeited by law.

Prior to this, a secret hiding place was discovered at Chideock Mill by the local Riding Officer when he searched the miller's living quarters in 1820. He discovered brandy and genever. The miller put the blame on his servant boy, but the truth came out when the miller's brother disappeared. Guilty by action, it seems.

The Weymouth Tax Collector reported, in 1804, that between Portland and Burton Hive beach, casks were, 'sunk on rafts till a convenient opportunity offers for taking them up' indicating that hiding incoming kegs of brandy and wine beneath the waves was a regular habit, while the officers at Poole reported a similar observation in 1813, stating, 'The number of casks usually landed in this manner is from twenty to forty.'

The last known Dorset smuggling run of our period was at Chideock in 1882. Sam Bartlett was an old-hand smuggler aged 69. The usual signals were made to a French vessel offshore and the smugglers pushed off in their small boat to collect the cargo. Taking longer than intended, they rowed to Eype Mouth, near West Bay. The cliffs are steep there, and their lookout fell and injured himself. Some tubs were landed, but the coastguard were now on their way so the smugglers smashed open the casks and drank the contents – one man consumed so much that it killed him.

The rest of the haul was deliberately sunk near Seatown, the intention being to collect it when opportunity presented itself. Unfortunately, this was not until several months had passed. Whether the tubs that were finally collected still contained good French brandy, or tasted more of seawater is not known. It had taken over six months and five different attempts to land the liquor. A somewhat disappointing finale to the 'romance' of Dorset smuggling.

The seaside town of Weymouth has the dubious accolade of being the port where the Black Death was brought into England in June 1348, but Dorset itself – aside from its smugglers – is known for the Jurassic Coast fossils, dinosaur remains, stunning scenery and the location for J. M. Falkner's novel, *Moonfleet*.

Published in 1898 the tale is set amid a fishing community where the protagonist, John Trenchard, becomes unwittingly embroiled with smugglers and is forced to flee from England. All comes right in the end, of course, but it is the telling of the tale that brings the excitement.

One of the charms of the story is Falkner's knowledge of the local geography. Moonfleet, the village, is East Fleet near Chesil Beach, while the headland of the fictional Snout, is Portland Bill.

(It was on this Dorset beach at Eype Mouth, near West Bay, overlooked by the famous Golden Cap, that I planned the outline plot for the first of my *Sea Witch Voyages*.)

Lyme Bay Eype Mouth and Golden Cap, Dorset. (©Tony Smith)

What the West Country smugglers lacked, according to popular belief regarding the need for violence, they made up for with their cunning, quick wits and knowledge of the sea and landscape. With many coves, sandy beaches and the loneliness of a rugged, uninhabited coast and the vast, empty and often fog-bound moors, Cornwall and Devon were a smuggler's paradise. With few men of the revenue, customs or militia on hand to enforce the law, smuggling was relatively easy. Add in the many representatives of the law who enjoyed the perks of contraband, then those smugglers who were caught were usually acquitted or treated with extreme leniency.

Having said that, it is probable that the West Country smuggler was as capable of violence as any Sussex or Kentishman, and the belief that the only damage caused was to the government's coffers is not strictly accurate. The reality is that, being more remote and further away from London, the West Country 'Gentlemen' did not receive such a bad press in the scandal-loving newssheets of the period. It is a fact that is almost as much alive today as it was back then. Where I live in North Devon crime is a thing we like to believe belongs to the big towns, although rural crime – stealing farming implements from a simple strimmer to an expensive tractor – is not uncommon. Sheep or cattle rustling is as much a crime as smuggling contraband, and in the 1700–1800s both were offences which, if the perpetrator was caught, would end at the gallows. The West Country, however, was – is – vastly different to the south-east.

Chapter Thirteen

The South-East

Hampshire, Wiltshire, Kent and Sussex

The West Country and Dorset were not the only counties to host smugglers. Where there were lonely stretches of coast, few inhabitants and beaches or creeks suitable for landing a cargo, there would be the secretive contraband runs and the infamous characters of the Free Trade. The nature of the smuggling, if not the goods, was different, however, and there were quite a few notable characters in the south-east who led lives that are difficult to separate as fact from fiction …

Hampshire, with its rivers, mudflats and ruinous castles attracted the smugglers. Close to France, close to London, not so many rough and rocky beaches that could so easily sink a boat. For the revenue, keeping a watch on the sea and the coast was a nigh-on impossible task, for the crossing from the Isle of Wight, only a few miles away from the mainland, was quick and easy, and any warning signals of potential trouble could be instantly seen by any crew in a boat.

Beaulieu River's western shore was made dangerous for the unsuspecting by miles of mudflats, well noted by the local smugglers who would use planks strapped to their feet to avoid sinking, but which formed sticky traps for the revenue. Brandy Hole, where tubs were temporarily sunk, became a local name for Pitt's Deep Hard, a jetty along one of the few navigable creeks.

The Beaulieu River itself formed a route for moving contraband many miles inland, the thick woodland and scattered farmsteads along its banks providing privacy for landing the goods. One story tells of a servant girl at a farm being questioned by a stranger about smuggling activities. She replied with feigned innocence: 'Why sir, we be abed by nine'. Later, she discovered that the man was a close friend of her master, and was testing her reliability. Another clear case of confirming Kipling's poem:

> You be careful what you say, and mindful what is said.
> If they call you 'pretty maid,' and chuck you 'neath the chin,
> Don't you tell where no one is, nor yet where no one's been!

Little Known Fact:
One village was nicknamed 'lazy town' because its residents were so often asleep during the day – they had been too busy smuggling all night!

Because it was frequently unoccupied Palace House, Beaulieu, was utilised as a convenient storehouse assisted by a variety of ghostly apparitions and noises which were manufactured by the smugglers to keep people away. Many of these made-up tales account for the present-day ghost stories connected with Beaulieu. Another prestigious place was Hurst Castle, also used for storing contraband – despite it being manned by revenue officers garrisoned there.

Now an unsightly oil refinery, Fawley's Ashlett Creek suited smugglers very well as Sprat's Down Wood stored the contraband. However, the villagers quickly earned themselves the derogatory title of 'Lazy Town' because they were all asleep during daylight hours. But then, their nocturnal activities were not much mentioned to counter the sarcasm.

The coastline of Kent varies between mud-based tidal creeks in the north, chalk cliffs and sandy bays in the east, with marshes and shingle beaches to the south. The gangs, comprising of ex-soldiers and Royal Navy sailors, fishermen, farm labourers and tradesmen of all sorts, were no strangers to blackmail, threatening violence and committing robbery, torture and murder – in addition to smuggling contraband that is. So confident were they in their strength and dominance that many of the more powerful Kent gangs transported their contraband by daylight protected by armed men, over distances of many miles.

According to government records, it was estimated in 1782 that more than a quarter of all vessels used for smuggling came from Kent and Sussex. More than half of the gin that came illegally into Britain was landed in Kent. The town of Deal came into its own during the Napoleonic Wars, but prior to that had always had a reputation for The Trade. A cavalry force was sent to search the town in 1781, but alerted to the raid, the townsfolk re-loaded their boats and sent everything they had secreted away back to France.

Determined to stop the Deal smuggling, in 1784 Prime Minister William Pitt, the 'Younger' ordered every boat that had been hauled up on the beach for over-wintering to be destroyed. The locals did not realise what was happening until it was too late to do anything except watch their livelihood go up in smoke and flames. Such was the resilience of the smuggling trade, and the profit made from it, new boats were soon acquired and business continued as usual.

Little Known Fact:
Many smugglers used nicknames instead of their real
names so that their identity would not be inadvertently
given away to the revenue men.

Based in the village of Groombridge, a few miles west of Tunbridge Wells and rising to the fore in the 1730s, the Groombridge Gang brought their contraband ashore at Fairlight, Lydd, Bulverhythe and Pevensey. Several of them had wonderful nicknames such as 'Yorkshire George', 'The Miller', 'Old Joll', 'Towzer', 'Flushing Jack' and my favourite, 'Nasty Face'. Nicknames, commonly used among smugglers and highwaymen, served a special purpose, not for terms of friendship – they hid true identities.

The gang was first mentioned in 1733 when thirty men were bringing a cargo of tea inland using fifty horses. A group of eager militiamen challenged them, but finding themselves outnumbered, were disarmed and forcibly marched en route at gunpoint until the cargo was delivered. An inconvenience for both sides, for the whole affair lasted four hours and ended at Lamberhurst where the militiamen were set free, unharmed but on oath not to renew their annoying interfering. The gang's apparent goodwill depreciated however, for in 1737 they were terrorising the area and it was necessary for the military to put a stop to them, initially without much success.

In 1740 the gang was involved in an organised attack at Robertsbridge, Sussex, along with the much-feared Hawkhurst Gang, but the gang's raids became more difficult after an anonymous informer, calling himself (or herself!) 'Goring', gave details of the gang's intentions, while another informer's tattling led to their arrest at the end of the 1740s. This latter traitor also informed on the Hooe Gang, which operated nearer the coast. I wonder who the informer was? A disgruntled gang member perhaps?

Little Known Fact
Illegal goods were sold quite openly at Faversham's Guildhall, with Daniel Defoe reporting, after he visited the town in 1724, that owling – wool smuggling – was as rife as ever it had been.

Further along the coast of Kent, Thanet has a quarry known as The Smuggler's Leap, which was immortalised by a short piece written in the *History of Thanet* by the Rev. Samuel Pegge. According to the tale, a riding officer was killed while chasing a smuggler in thick fog. Going at a gallop both men forgot about the quarry and hurtled over the edge.

The ghosts of the two men and their horses are still there... if you happen to see one, or any ghostly smuggler, do let me know.

Not all tales are amusing, however. Smuggling was a serious business, especially for the Owlers of Romney Marsh. It is estimated that by 1689, more than 480,000lbs of wool was being smuggled, per annum, to France from Romney Marsh via the expertise of the 'owlers'. Troops were sent in 1693 in an attempt to end the trade, with a riot breaking out at Rye, East Sussex, in 1696. The attempt did not accomplish much because smuggling was common right along the Sussex coast with the majority of contraband being carried overnight to London by pack ponies.

Rye, in Sussex, was one of the ancient Cinque Ports, coastal towns in Kent and Sussex, originally designated for trade and military matters. The 'five ports' were Hastings, New Romney, Hythe, Dover and Sandwich. Rye used to be a subsidiary of New Romney, but became a Cinque Port when storms and excessive silting put an end to New Romney as a viable harbour. Rye is a charming town, now, due to land reclamation schemes, three miles inland from the sea, with cobbled streets and houses that stand cheek to cheek up against each other, making use of shared cellars and attics. The Hawkhurst Gang (them again!) frequented the Mermaid Inn, without fear of being intercepted by the revenue – possibly the fact that they kept their loaded pistols in full view had something to do with this! They would assure their safety by firing the pistols into the air, pointing them at passers-by and shouting 'Bang!' One young man, James Marshall, became too nosey regarding their business. Soon after, he mysteriously disappeared and was never seen again.

Several Rye inns were associated with all sorts of different smugglers: the Red Lion, The Flushing Inn and the London Trader's

Mermaid Street, Rye, where many a smuggler must have trod. (©Tomasz ZieLinski)

The romance of Romney Marsh, where miles of windswept open space made surprise attacks by the excise men or rival gangs an unlikely threat. (©Helen Hotson)

Inn which was connected by Traders Passage to the lookout point in Watchbell Street. Rye's cunning boat builders produced vessels suitable for the Trade, incorporating concealed hiding places for contraband, such as boats within boats, where there was a gap left between the two hulls, an inner and outer, for secret storage. For an idea of what a smuggling town used to be like – visit Rye.

Lydd was a smuggling centre in the 1700s, although not a safe place for those who went against the Gentlemen. William Carter had arrested some owlers, but they were bailed by the local magistrate. Master Carter and his men were then attacked by fifty armed men in revenge. Not all men of the law were honest: Lydd's Dragoons in the 1730s made for themselves a nice profit from seized brandy by selling it at two shillings per half-anker.

Dymchurch, the setting for the classic *Dr Syn* novels by Russell Thorndike, does not retain much of its historical charm now, while Hythe, one of the Cinque Ports, is a very pretty town and its Red Lion

Coaching Inn pops up in the novels, while the Smuggler's Retreat speaks for itself. The Bell Inn had an underground stream, ideal for floating in barrels and keeping them safe by attaching them to hooks dangling from the cellar's ceiling.

Nearly all Romney Marsh towns boast (probably fictional) tunnels linking houses, inns, hiding places or routes to the sea. It would be nice to find one of these illusive hiding places. There again, Romney Marsh itself is very evocative, so the mysteries of the Marsh make up for any shortfall where tunnels are concerned.

One of Hampshire's most notable smuggling characters was Tom Johnstone of Lymington. He was born in 1772, was reputedly extremely handsome, with vivid blue eyes, of admirable physique and over 6ft tall. By the age of 12, he had mastered seamanship taught to him by his fisherman and smuggler father. By 15 he was a smuggler himself. He had many adventures working for the French and English, was injured and imprisoned more than once – and escaped each time. At 21 he became a privateer against France during one of the many wars, was caught by the French, negotiated his release as a potential spy, but was recaptured by the British press gang at Southampton. He deserted the Navy, was named an outlaw and returned to smuggling. In 1798 he was again captured, but again escaped by bribing the turnkey at Winchelsea gaol, and fled to the Netherlands.

As cheeky as ever, a year later he became a Royal Navy pilot with the remit of booting the French out of Holland, earning for himself a reward of £1,000 and a free pardon. Pride before a fall. In 1802 he was substantially in debt for living too lavishly in London and found himself a debtor in Fleet Street gaol.

You've guessed it. He escaped. Not, however, without incident, for he was injured while doing so. He took himself to France to recover and joined the Guinea Run, smuggling gold from England for Napoleon's campaigns. Unpatriotic maybe, but at least Johnstone refused an offer by Napoleon himself to lead a French naval invasion against England. The result was nine months in a French Prison, his escape not being so easy this time.

He then resided in New Orleans, America, for a while but joined with inventor, Robert Fulton, who was working on making the first limpet mines. An initial attempt to use them in 1806 to blow up French vessels failed, but another was successful in 1809.

Once again Johnstone became a turncoat when he took the position of commander of a revenue cutter, HMS *Fox*, earning himself lasting hatred from his previous fellow smugglers. Retiring at the age of 44 with a Navy pension he dabbled in another of Fulton's inventions, submarines, but almost drowned during a demonstration of the first under-water vessel, the *Nautilus*.

He finally died, peacefully, at 67. All that would make a splendid adventure novel, although maybe difficult to believe, but sometimes fact *is* stranger than fiction!

Chapter Fourteen

The East Coast

Essex, Norfolk, Suffolk and the North-East

Across the North Sea, Holland and Flanders was a mere 100 miles away from England's east coast. The Little Boats of south-east England made the crossing during the crisis of Dunkirk near the start of the Second World War, and if hundreds of these small fishing boats could make the trip, (in many cases, more than one voyage,) under the fire of Nazi Germany, think how easy it would have been for experienced smugglers to sail across in the 1700s. You would think that the Fens of Norfolk and Suffolk would, therefore, be packed with smugglers…

The river Thames, the direct route into London from the North Sea, was not the most suitable way to bring contraband goods to Britain's capital, especially when there was the adequate alternative of Essex, so named from the East Saxons who settled in the fifth and sixth centuries. Foulness Island and the mudflats of Southend were not forgiving for men who did not know the channels and tides, while the network of Essex dykes and the frequent mists and fogs, to those 'in the know', provided secretive routes inbound. There are more than fifty suitable rivers and creeks dotted along the Essex coastline, making it almost impossible for the early revenue men to patrol with any efficiency.

In his guide to 'Marsh Country Rambles', published in 1904, Herbert W. Tompkins writes of the men searching for smugglers: 'There are well defined rivers, creeks or outfalls; to search the coast for some notorious gang on a dark night was like looking for the proverbial needle in a haystack.' He adds, 'The Preventive Officer could see nothing unless actually on the wall in which case if there was enough light to serve his purpose it also served to render him a conspicuous mark for a bullet.'

Although the long arm of the law was not always a danger – Hezekiah Staines, a local constable, carried out his policeman's duties by day, and became a smuggler by night. Brandy Bridge at Tillingham, and Brandy Hole along the river Crouch, are reminders of the activities of the past, and, so rumour has it, to the southeast of Maldon there is still a batch of Dutch genever hidden in a cache somewhere in Asheldham Woods ... don't rush to grab a spade, I doubt it tastes very nice now!

The Crouch and Blackwater are isolated stretches of water, even in the bustling twenty-first century. Inlets and creeks criss-cross the surrounding marshland, and with the land lying so low, lanterns placed on the few high points, such as Beacon Hill, could be clearly seen as prearranged markers on clear nights. The church of St Peter at Bradwell was a favoured storage place for contraband, while the landlord at the nearby Green Man tavern would have served many a pint of ale to smugglers making their plans to sail across to Holland, and would have benefited from their return trips. Rochford's church tower provided a secure hiding place for our pre-1900s smugglers, while the nearby village of Paglesham boasted (although quietly), that nearly everyone who lived there had something to do with smuggling.

East Anglia is a name with a direct link to the East Angles, who in the fifth century along with the East Saxons, migrated from what is now Germany, Flanders and Jutland. Norfolk and Suffolk link to the 'North Folk' and the 'South Folk'. Even today those lonely Fens that saw the Saxons' boats sail in (and much later, the Vikings), have meandering creeks and rivers that are known only to local residents.

The Reverend Forbes Phillips wrote *The Romance Of Smuggling* under the name of Atholl Forbes in the early 1900s, in which he recounted several smuggling tales about the Yarmouth area, including those connected to the past history of his own vicarage which had vast cellars and, reputedly, tunnels connecting to the waterways. One of the yarns relates Corton Cliff which was used as a landing place for contraband. A group of smugglers encountered a preventative officer spying on them, they apprehended him, stuffed his head down a rabbit hole and pinioned him there by hammered a stake into the ground between his legs and through his breeches. I would wager that the poor man was terrified – I wonder how long he remained there before being found, and how much teasing he received afterwards?

The revenue men were based at Yarmouth, the opening to the vast waterways of the Norfolk Broads, but as usual their task of stopping the smugglers was something of a forlorn hope. Two methods were undertaken by the Free Traders, one was for the contraband to be sunk beneath the water for local fishermen to retrieve later along with their lobster and crab pots, the other, especially further along the coast, was to wait for the tide to ebb – and along these wide, flat beaches it ebbed a long way – then simply toss the kegs and waterproofed packets and bundles over the side for the local folk to collect in their carts along with gathering the seaweed kelp, and digging for cockles and mussels. Any preventative man venturing out on to the wet sand would be spotted easily, enough time for any contraband to 'disappear'.

The Parson Woodforde public house at Weston Longville, not far from Norwich, commemorates Parson James Woodforde who obtained his living in the parish in 1774. The pub was originally built as a private residence in 1827 but was converted to an inn, named the Five Ringers in 1845 – so called because it was opposite the church and the bell ringers would always drop in for a pint or two after their work was done. (A tradition that still continues!)

Parson Woodforde, however, is not remembered for the church bells or his fondness for downing ale, fine claret and port accompanied by a generous feast for himself and his guests. His legacy is the detailed diaries which he kept for over forty-five years. He gives a wonderful view of everyday life in the eighteenth century – including the mention of smuggling. He was in the main only a receiver of goods, as far as we know, although maybe he omitted to include any further deeds beyond the packets of tea, bottles of gin and kegs of brandy that he purchased. In March 1777 he recorded:

> Andrews the smuggler brought me this night about
> 11 o'clock a bag of Hyson Tea 6 Pd weight. He frightened
> us a little by whistling under the parlour window just as we
> were going to bed. I gave him some Geneva and paid for the
> tea at 10/6 a Pd.

Woodforde bought contraband from Richard Andrews, Hewitt from Mattishall Burgh, the Honingham blacksmith and a man called 'Moonshine' – Robert Buck. He was also a client of a few who did not wish to be named for he records that one night a knock at his door revealed no one to be there, save for a few kegs of alcohol.

Archives from the 1783 *Norfolk Chronicle* supply much of our knowledge, with several of the snippets of information being extremely interesting. In September 1783, one local gang of 200 men dropped anchor near the village of Thornham, near Hunstanton, at nine of the clock in the morning and brought their contraband ashore, a task which lasted into the early afternoon. Several preventative officers were watching, but were powerless to do anything because they were outnumbered and poorly armed.

It does make you wonder if that was nothing more than a convenient excuse. Maybe the revenue men were encouraged to, figuratively, 'watch the wall' while 'the Gentlemen went by'? It is not hard to imagine those king's men, disillusioned by their job, poorly paid and armed, sitting idly smoking their pipes, muskets un-primed, enjoying a pleasant day in the sunshine while watching the smugglers toil up and down the beach. Or maybe that day was stormy, a wind lashing the sea, whipping the sand to sting eyes and leave a bad taste in the mouth. Far better for those few, undermanned revenue men to sit in the shelter of the dunes, especially in exchange for a couple of packets of 'baccy, or some kegs of brandy that conveniently 'fell off the back of a donkey'.

The *Norfolk Chronicle* also reported in November 1783, that a troop of the 15th Regiment of Light Dragoons arrived at Lynn (now King's Lynn) to make use of the town as their winter quarters. Their aim was to assist the revenue officers against the smuggling gangs.

I doubt the townsfolk were particularly overjoyed at having an entire regiment keeping its eye on what boats came and went.

The revenue men were still struggling, however. In 1780 excise officers, Messrs Brock, Carter, Mason and others, managed to seize something in the order of 1,500 gallons of rum, brandy and genever near Huntingford. The smugglers attacked the revenue men but were beaten off, while in 1783 at Cromer a smuggler's cutter, in difficulties because of poor weather, was approached by excise men and soldiers intent on seizing it and the crew. Things did not go to plan; while attempting to board the boat note had not been taken of the gale-force wind, driving rain or rough seas. Sadly several king's men were drowned in consequence.

For the north-east coast of England, there is a long history of trade with Sweden, Denmark, Norway and the Netherlands, (and invasion in the form of the Vikings). Holland especially had several trade links both legal and illegal. Wool was one of the first commodities to be smuggled from northern English harbours such as Humberside, Whitby and York, with wool soon replaced by the importation of gin.

Hull in the late 1500s had forty-three different wharves belonging to various merchants where goods could be loaded and unloaded, making the task of overseeing in-bound and outbound trade an almost impossible task. It was not until 1775 that the customs' repeated pleas for one continuous wharf to be built was finally achieved.

Remote and sparsely populated you would think that from East Anglia up to Humberside would be ideal smuggling country, but oddly, there are few official records and even fewer local tales. Either the smugglers along the east coast were experts at avoiding the revenue men, and the locals were very good at keeping quiet where gossip was concerned, or, as is more likely, this part of England was not especially smuggling territory.

Even with our modern road systems driving to anywhere along the east coast, once the M11 or M1 are left behind, is taken at a leisurely pace. It is more likely that because of the lack of tracks and roads, very few not especially highly populated towns and widely scattered, small villages there was no practicality for the large smuggling gangs.

Contraband once run in had to be dispersed and delivered quickly and easily. A handsome profit had to be made. Once the waterways of Norfolk and Suffolk, and higher up into Lincolnshire, were left behind there was nowhere for the smugglers to go within a swift couple of miles walk or cart ride, and outside of a few notable rich men, or local villagers, no one of note to sell the contraband to.

Chapter Fifteen

Wales, Isle of Man, Ireland and Scotland

Cardiff, in the south of Wales, was once a remote harbour and nearby Sully Island and Swanbridge have court records revealing that 28,000lb of cheese and eighty barrels of butter were seized as contraband in 1569. Further official records for Wales and the North-West coast of England are rare to find, alas, because of a fire in 1815 at the Custom House in London, which destroyed most of the documentation. However, there is no reason to believe that there was no smuggling in these areas, or is there?

Little Known Fact:
Salt was the most lucrative cargo smuggled from
Ireland – from Scotland it was whisky.

Goods smuggled from Europe might not have been practical, but anything coming from Ireland was easy to bring in. The 'Troubles' in Ireland in the latter part of the seventeenth century meant a ban on shipping, so legitimate cargoes were hard to come by in the West and Wales. Enter the smugglers. Salt was one of the primary cargoes because of heavy taxation – and Ireland was a substantial source for rock salt. Ireland was also useful as a staging post for goods brought across from the Americas, particularly during the War of Independence.

Cumbria's court records give evidence of sentences for smuggling, although the Fells did not lend themselves to efficient transportation. Cumbria was ideally located for the Isle of Man, however, which entertained a major source of smuggled goods because of its situation of being outside of English Crown Law. King Henry IV granted a freedom of trade charter to the island in 1405. In 1704 Parliament banned all trade with France, but it did not apply to Manx vessels, so a back-door route to smuggle brandy and wine into England was left open.

Cumbria being so close to Scotland's border also brings an anomaly where a lack of evidence for smuggling is concerned, especially given that the smuggling of illegally distilled whisky was common. One explanation is that it was more profitable to sail direct from Scottish landing places, therefore by-passing Cumbria's ragged terrain. This does seem to be the case, as several reports mention the prolific amount of small boats from Ireland and the Isle of Man plying to and from Scotland, with a substantial number being seized at sea and impounded for carrying contraband.

In Scotland itself, the most lucrative commodities to be smuggled was whisky (spelt whiskey, with an 'e' in Ireland and the USA). Dated to 1618 there is a reference to 'uiskie' in the funeral account of a Highland laird, and a letter to the Earl of Mar from 1622 mentioning the spirit. Written by Sir Duncan Campbell of Glenorchy, he reported that officers sent to Glenorchy had been given the best entertainment, for they 'wanted not [for] wine nor *aquavite*.'

'Aqua vitae', the Water of Life – whisky – formed part of the rent paid for Highland farms, was appreciated during long winters, and provided a welcome to guests. However, its popularity attracted the attention of the Scottish Parliament and the first taxes on the sale of whisky were introduced in 1644, fixing the duty at 2*s* 8*d* (13p) or roughly about £40 in today's equivalent, per pint, (the Scots pint being approximately one third of a gallon.) This, inevitably, resulted in a rise of distilling, and smuggling, illicit whisky.

Part of the agreement of the Union between Scotland and England in 1707 was that English taxes would not be enforced north of the border, but in 1724 Parliament introduced a tax which caused riots in Scotland, and distillers were driven further underground. These distillers and their comrade smugglers saw no reason to pay for making whisky, especially with such a substantial market for selling it. Government agents were confiscating around 10,000 stills per annum, but the smuggling trade was barely affected.

By 1780, there were only eight legal distilleries and well over 400 illegal ones. Smugglers organised signalling systems to warn of approaching excise men, and smuggling whisky had become a standard practice which lasted for over 150 years. Every conceivable storage space was used to hide the liquor, including using coffins for transportation. This eventually prompted the Duke of Gordon, on whose land some of the finest illicit whisky in Scotland was being distilled, to propose in the House of Lords that it should be made profitable to produce whisky legally. So, in 1823 the Excise Act eased the restrictions on licensed distilleries while making it harder for illegal stills to operate. It sanctioned the distilling of whisky in return for a licence fee of £10, and a set payment per gallon. Smuggling whisky almost completely died out within a few short months as it was no longer worthwhile.

For elsewhere, however, local smuggling must have been a lucrative side-line for anyone who cared to go out in a boat, or trundle a few kegs of brandy from the coast to the nearest tavern or town, except, unlike the south and west of England, smuggling would not have been quite as prolific given the distance from the European countries to the shores of Wales and Scotland, and the difficulties of the currents and tides that border the west of the British Isles.

Chapter Sixteen

The Smuggler's Rest
(or Pausing for a Tot or Two of Brandy)

There is a romantic ideal that surrounds smuggling and smugglers, at least as far as the perceived 'jolly' fellows of the past are concerned. For the smugglers of the seventeenth and eighteenth centuries we tend to shrug aside the fact that they were, all of them, from fisherman to country gent, lawbreakers. Except how many of us tend to, occasionally, break the law by speeding, or paying the gardener in cash to avoid declaring the tax? Minor things, but to smugglers covertly bringing in a few kegs of brandy, or packets of tobacco, this was equally as minor. For the landlords of taverns, inns, pubs and other such similar hostelries, smuggling came in very useful. Are all the tales of 'Smuggler's Rest' inns factual though?

The excitement of the fictional side of smuggling, especially during the Victorian and Edwardian era, led to a rise of claims for association for seaside resorts with smugglers. With the Victorian popularity of 'taking the sea air' and sea bathing escalating, the need for places of natural or scientific interest and 'folklore adventures' to be visited, such fashionable vacation trips rose higher, especially once travel was made easier by the opening of the railways and construction of better roads. Visitors to the coast needed somewhere to stay, and taverns and inns with an extra 'marketing angle' kindly obliged.

Conveniently disregarding the criminal element, hotels, inns and hostelries in most towns along the eastern, southern and West Country coasts took advantage of any smuggling connections by highlighting the romantic side of the past. Some towns and individual inns along stretches of coast even vied with each other for who could boast the most sinister, daring, notorious or dastardly smuggling gangs. The

'Smuggler's Inn' and 'Smuggler's Rest' became the most popular names when rebranding coastal taverns. If the inn also had access to a secluded cove and a dark cellar, all the better. The sad thing is that many a pub, so titled, probably never saw a single smuggler.

The pubs, taverns and inns served as meeting places for smugglers, with the landlords being clients for the contraband liquor. Dominated by the Hawkhurst Gang, in 1747 the Star and Eagle Inn at Goudhurst in Kent was a haunt of these ruffians. The landlord probably welcomed their custom but the resident villagers did not appreciate their horses and carts being frequently commandeered. There is no evidence beyond general belief, but the Oak and Ivy Inn, also in Kent, was supposedly the Hawkhurst Gang's main headquarters. Although the present building apparently does not seem to have carried a licence as an alehouse prior to the mid-1800s, well after the gang's operational days. Could there have been a different Oak and Ivy Inn, there previously, one now long gone?

In addition to serving as inns, taverns or public houses doubled as makeshift mortuaries and hospitals for the smugglers' rivals, the revenue men. And for magistrate's courts when the smugglers were caught and brought to trial.

Not all tavern landlords were involved with smuggling, but those who were often made a good job – and a fortune – from dabbling in the Free Trade. One such man was Master Isaac Gulliver Junior, born in 1745 and who carried on the family's smuggling interest from his father, Isaac senior. A customs officer in 1788 recorded that Isaac (junior) was a person of 'great speculating genius'.

After marriage to Elizabeth Beale in 1768, Isaac took over his father-in-law's tavern, the Blacksmith's Arms at Thorney Down on the road from Blandford to Salisbury in Wiltshire. He changed the name to the King's Arms and took full advantage of the road being one of the major smuggling routes. He soon had about fifty men in his employ, and was cunning in his exploits, even down to purchasing an ancient earthwork, Eggardon Hill, in 1776, which, by planting trees atop its ridge, he used as a suitable landmark to guide in smugglers' boats.

In 1782, he took the government amnesty against smugglers by agreeing to provide two men to serve in the Royal Navy. According to the customs officials, Gulliver then discontinued smuggling tea and spirits but continued to smuggle wine, a fact which they appear to have very conveniently ignored.

The Forge Hammer Inn in Hampshire once stood at Sowley Pond. Frequently smugglers hid contraband in the cellars, but so the story goes, one night the revenue came a-nosing and to give the smugglers time to shift the contraband to a different hiding place, the landlady accosted one of the leading officers for not paying his due debts for refreshment consumed. By the time she had finished berating him the cellars were empty of anything that should not have been there.

Little Known Fact:
The King's Head tavern at Grafty Green, near
Maidstone in Kent, regularly saw a smuggler named
Dover Bill and his gang. When the revenue interrupted
the smugglers' drinking one evening a full-scale battle
erupted. All the gang members were arrested and
hanged, except for Bill who managed to escape, but
now had no colleagues to work with.

As well as being convenient meeting places where smugglers could discuss 'business' (of varying kinds) many individual landlords financed smuggling runs, particularly where spirits, brandy, gin, wine and such were concerned as they could easily sell the supplied liquor over the counter for a cheaper outlay and larger profit.

Tide, erosion and the centuries between then and now have altered the shape of the coastline of Sussex and at Crowlink, where there are now cliffs, back in the 1700s there was a cart gap which the smugglers made good use of. Giving suitable access to the sea, and frequented by most of the East Sussex smuggling gangs, contraband was hauled ashore from beached vessels, and thus Crowlink gave its name to a highly prized smuggled liquor.

Eventually, 'Genuine Crowlink' became a by-word brand name for illicit gin, with printed labels even being displayed openly on kegs and barrels.

Alfriston's Market Cross House, renamed Ye Olde Smugglers Inn, stands in the centre of the town a handful of miles to the north-east of Seaford. The place, like many another tavern, was frequented by smugglers. With a maze of passageways, over twenty rooms, several staircases and fifty different doors, it admirably leant itself to various illicit goings-on. Tunnels were believed to have been used, although there is no evidence to support this.

Stanton Collins was the local gang leader, and he made good use of this confusing house. No one from his gang was ever arrested, although the Collins' gang came to an abrupt end when their leader was arrested and transported – not for smuggling, but for sheep rustling.

Five or so miles north-east of Eastbourne, Sussex, Thorpe Cottage sits opposite the pub at the village of Jevington. Nearby Birling Gap has fallen prey to extensive erosion, but back in the 1700s the Jevington Smugglers brought their contraband ashore here, as well as making use of nearby Crowlink – and the 'Genuine Crowlink' brand liquor. Led by James Petit, known also as 'Jevington Jig', master Petit had a variety of occupations aside from his initial trade of innkeeper and professional smuggler.

He dallied in informing, horse stealing, general thievery and other 'roguish pursuits'. When his inn was surrounded by the revenue men, he donned women's clothes and rushed outside in a bid to escape. He scuppered his intention, though, as he forgot to change his heavy boots for something more feminine beneath his lace-edged petticoats. In 1792 he turned his loyalty around and assisted the revenue men with seizing a haul of contraband tobacco.

Situated in East Sussex, Hooe boasts the Red Lion Inn, which was the headquarters of the Hooe Gang. The present-day lime trees are supposedly a remnant of an old smuggler's signal; so legend has it, lime trees signify a safe place for smugglers to bring their contraband and take their ease.

Whether this is true or not is unknown. I will leave you to ponder an answer, perhaps while enjoying a pint of ale or a tot of Genever and tonic at your local pub. Has it got any lime trees outside?

Was Jamaica Inn really a smugglers' pub?

Lady Browning – Dame Daphne du Maurier DBE, wrote several much-loved novels, including *Rebecca, Frenchman's Creek* and *Jamaica Inn*.

Little Known Fact:
Daphne du Maurier had the idea for *Jamaica Inn* after being stranded on Bodmin Moor.

The real Jamaica Inn (and therefore the fictional one as well) is high on the wild and rugged Bodmin Moor in Cornwall, situated beside the A30 midway between Launceston and Bodmin. There was an older, sixteenth century building, but Jamaica Inn was rebuilt in 1750 and extended in 1778. It originally stood on its own with nothing else nearby and was a coaching inn – a stopping-off point for travellers journeying to or from Cornwall to Bristol, Bath, London and beyond – an eighteenth-century equivalent to a motorway service station. Then, as now, it must have been a relief to see the lights of the inn glowing in the distance on a wet, windy night. Crossing Bodmin Moor, even within the comfort of a modern car, can be somewhat daunting when the mist, heavy rain or high winds close in. Not to mention the snow…

Some regular visitors of the past were welcomed – secretly under the cover of darkness as Jamaica Inn was indeed a real smuggler's 'halfway house', an exchange point for contraband brought ashore along the Cornish coast to be transferred to carts taking the goods further into England. Once on its way to London, Oxford, or wherever, there was no chance of the authorities tracing its origin, or those who had smuggled the contraband in.

Often thought to refer to the smuggled Jamaica rum stored in the cellars, the name, *Jamaica Inn* is more likely to trace back to the inn's original landowners, the Trelawney family, two of whom were Governors of Jamaica.

Edward Trelawny was born in Trelawne, Cornwall, in 1699. In 1738 he was appointed Governor of Jamaica. He was openly against slavery, publishing a controversial pamphlet in 1747 where he spoke out against the obnoxious trade. Given that Jamaica, and much of the English and Colonial economy at the time depended on slaves, he dared not champion abolition itself, knowing that he could then risk his position as governor and any chance of taking a seat in Parliament. However, the fight of putting an end to the actual barbarity of the Trade, seemed a suitable compromise.

In 1751 he married a widow who held a considerable Jamaican-made fortune and because of ill health, left office in 1752 and returned to Cornwall. He died in January 1754, with his estate passing to his elder brother, John. But what about the inn? There is a question mark over which of the two brothers founded and therefore named it. John or Edward?

If Jamaica Inn, probably the most famous smugglers' inn, is connected to *Edward* Trelawny it makes a very fine memorial to his name and deeds.

Daphne du Maurier's famous *Jamaica Inn*. (©Alexa Zari)

The tale of how *Jamaica Inn* came to be written is as fascinating as the novel itself. The young Daphne and a companion became lost in heavy mist while riding on Bodmin Moor, and their horses took them to safety by heading towards the inn. While recovering from her fright, the local rector diverted Daphne's attention by telling her stories of smugglers, which sparked her writer's imagination.

The story concerns 23-year-old Mary Yellan, who travels to live with her only surviving relative, her mother's sister Patience Merlyn, at Jamaica Inn. It does not take Mary long to work out that Patience's husband Joss is involved with wreckers, smugglers and murderers. Desperate to do the right thing she tells the local vicar of her suspicions … but to say more would spoil the story for any who have not read it.

> It was a cold grey day in late November. The weather had changed overnight, when a backing wind brought in a granite sky and a mizzling rain with it, and although it was now only a little after two o'clock of the afternoon the pallor of a winter evening seemed to have closed upon the hills, cloaking them in a mist. It would be dark by four.

Intriguing and evocative opening lines.

Jamaica Inn was published in 1936. The inspiration behind its conception sounds just as fictional as the novel but is, apparently, true. The inn is a real place, and it really was involved with smugglers. Whether many of the other taverns, inns and pubs claiming such a connection were Smuggler's Rests is quite another matter entirely.

Chapter Seventeen

On the Other Side of the Pond

Across the Atlantic, the American Colonies abounded as much as England with smuggling ventures. Smuggling was a way of resisting British domination so was, in part, also rebellion. The simplest way to smuggle was to trade goods in the harbours and ports along the Chesapeake or in the Caribbean. Ships, mainly Dutch, would drop anchor and sell their cargo to anyone who wanted to buy, the officials on duty operating a very blind eye or conveniently absent – when bribed, of course. And then there is the small matter of whether smuggling was the cause of a war …

Britain was determined that trade would only be between the Colonies and the UK and transported in British or Colonial ships. Goods had to be loaded or unloaded at British harbours so that duties went into British finance, and this monopoly extended to ensuring that all imported goods to America had to come from England. The British Government set the trade prices, and it did not take Americans long to realise that if goods were smuggled in and out, excessive duties could be side-stepped.

Little Known Fact:
In the seventeenth and eighteenth centuries, the
governors of some American Colonies received goods
obtained through piracy and smuggling.

In the Caribbean, Jamaica had its own share of smuggling, but not always at the expense of Britain. Before the rise of the eighteenth-century sugar plantations, Jamaica profited because of Spain's trade laws which prohibited no more than two Spanish fleets a year, and no foreign traders at all. Such regulations controlled the gold and silver but resulted in their colonial Spanish population craving the goods they needed. Smuggled trade from Jamaica supplied that need. The combination of smuggling and privateering, under the auspices of Captain Henry Morgan, made Port Royal so rich even the servants could afford fine clothes and frivolous trinkets. Dubbed the 'wickedest city in the world' because of the huge number of pirates there, the downfall came in the summer of 1692. An earthquake destroyed much of the town, thousands died and those who survived moved across the bay to build what is now Kingston.

Smuggling in North America, because of the vast rivers and stretches of coastline, was easy to do and difficult to prevent. As in England, incentives to encourage informers failed.

Tobacco and sugar were exported legally to Britain, rum and molasses were a smuggler's favourites, but from the late 1600s the most popular goods to be imported were luxury household items originating from the Dutch. Colonists were starting to make money from their plantations and estates, and they wanted grand houses which needed to be furnished – also in a grand style. The Dutch obliged by selling everything required at forty per cent less than the English traders.

The American Civil War of 1861–65 involved smuggling essential supplies, especially gunpowder, arms and ammunition, but there were some surprising items on the 'wish list' of smuggled goods. One of the most daring 'runs' was undertaken by four women in July 1864. To aid Confederate soldiers Elizabeth White, Kate and Betsie Ball and Annie Hempstone faced a charge of treason if caught. Their mission was to fetch desperately needed boots and clothing from the Union side of the Potomac River. They set about collecting what they needed, hiding the items beneath their hooped skirts. To the ladies' dismay, Union soldiers had arrived at the river's crossing point. The four women were forced to retreat to where Elizabeth White's mother lived, and hide the supplies in her house. The four were discovered and despite insistence that they were visiting for pleasure, were arrested and taken to the Old Capitol Prison, Washington DC.

The hooped skirt – who would believe that contraband was hidden beneath?
(©mantonino)

With no evidence to establish a charge of spying or smuggling, they were released after three weeks. Risking further arrest they returned to the house, hid the supplies beneath their skirts once again and headed home via Edward's Ferry. They reached Virginia unscathed, where the boots and clothes were distributed to grateful men. Brave ladies indeed. Modern fashions would not be as useful!

Let us backtrack from hooped skirts concealing contraband in the 1880s, to the previous century. In the mid-1700s American Colonists were beginning to have no interest in Britain's various European squabbles and the increasing customs duties served to enhance the British economy, not the American Treasury. Eventually, enough colonists saw the unfairness of this and acted against it.

From the mid-1600s into the early 1700s the Colonies were not regarded as very important to the British. The vast estates that would, in later years, become established for essential trade – cotton, tobacco, sugar – were not yet properly in existence, only the edges of what by the nineteenth century would be the United States, were inhabited by western white men. Virginia trade focused on the shores of the Chesapeake Bay; not until 1716 did Governor Alexander Spotswood venture as far as the Blue Ridge Mountains, and it was to be many more years before 'The West' was even discovered, let alone settled. Florida – the name is Spanish for 'the land of flowers' – back then in the 1500s included what would become the Carolinas and Georgia combined. Regarded as an empty land, in 1763, Spain saw no value in keeping it, so traded Florida to Britain in exchange for Havana and Cuba which were under British control. The Netherlands, too, gave up the swampy islands of what was New Amsterdam when surrendering to the English in 1664. It was renamed New York, after King Charles II's brother, James Duke of York.

As the 1750s and 1760s approached, Americans were becoming disgruntled with England, the English king, the English government and English trade laws. Tea was eventually to play a big part in this unhappiness. The American War of Independence, known as the American Revolutionary War to all Americans, occurred because of conflict of political differences, taxation imposed by King George III and the deterioration of relationships. While smuggling was not the main cause it played an enormous part – or rather, the intervention to end smuggling did.

One single ship was the reason behind the war. She is now known as HMS *Surprise*, from Patrick O'Brian's novel of the same name, and the movie *Master and Commander*. *Surprise* is a replica of her previous pre-movie persona, HMS *Rose*.

In the eighteenth century, *Rose* was a Royal Navy vessel sent in 1768 to prevent smuggling by patrolling the seas around Rhode Island. But the story is not quite as simple as that...

How did it all begin?

In the 1600s, colonists could only purchase imports from English sources. The French, meanwhile, passed a law to allow as much sugar as possible to be shipped to France, but outlawed their colonies from processing rum from the by-product, molasses. So the French sugarcane estates were amassing vast amounts of molasses with no idea of what to do with it. Then one planter hit on the plan of giving it away to the British Colonies. Good idea – except the governors of states such as Virginia declined because it was illegal. The Governor of Rhode Island was a wiser man. Elected by the islanders, not, like the others, appointed by the British, he could make his own decisions. So as much molasses as possible was imported into Rhode Island in order to make rum which could then be legally exported.

War with France put a fly in the ointment (or should that be in the rum?) because France controlled the main supplier, Haiti. Ah, there was a way round it! Cartels were special boats which repatriated prisoners of war. International agreement dictated that these prison-carrying cartels, which flew special flags of exemption, were to be left alone. It was also permitted for these cartels to acquire cargo for the return journey to offset the cost of returning prisoners. Designed to carry over 200 prisoners, vessels from Rhode Island frequently only had one or two aboard, some of whom had been deliberately 'captured' so that they could be exchanged for molasses. A good arrangement between Haiti and Rhode Island; it worked well.

King George III did not approve, so he renewed the Sugar Act of 1733. It was now becoming difficult for Rhode Islanders to continue with their covert molasses trade. To enforce the new law HMS *Squirrel* was dispatched in December 1763. She immediately confiscated the cargo of the Rhode Island merchant ship, *Rhoda*, but *Squirrel* transferred to a different patrol area the following January and *Rhoda* was re-seized by Rhode Islanders and returned to her owner. An outright act of defiance against Britain.

Another Royal Navy vessel was sent, the six-gun schooner, *Saint John*, commanded by 19-year-old Lieutenant Thomas Hill. *Saint John* stopped every smuggling ship that came into Newport harbour, which meant nearly every cargo was confiscated, the captains arrested, some of the crews set ashore with the rest press-ganged into service. Pressing men was legal in Britain but a law in 1707, during Queen Anne's reign, decreed that Americans were exempt in order to encourage people to emigrate to the Colonies. This law had been forgotten, except Rhode Island's governor, Stephen Hopkins, a self-taught lawyer, knew of it. On 9 July 1764 he went aboard *Saint John* and ordered Lieutenant Hill to depart. Hill refused and threatened to throw Hopkins overboard. Hopkins returned to shore, went straight to the fort on Goat Island and ordered the gunners to sink the *Saint John*. All the eighteen-pound cannons opened fire ... Hill cut the anchor cable and departed. This was the first hostility against Britain, a full twelve years before the Declaration of Independence.

King George III was furious. HMS *Maidstone* was sent to replace *Saint John*. Except, the citizens of Newport rowed out during the night, removed the crew at pistol-point and burned the ship. Another British ship arrived in 1769, the ironically named *Liberty*, which had been confiscated from her colonial owner John Hancock – a smuggler. She was also set ablaze. *Gaspee* came in 1772, ran aground in Narragansett Bay and was set on fire.

Because of the time it took to cross the Atlantic, it was several months before the British Government and Admiralty heard of these deeds.

They sent stern-worded letters of complaint, which also took months to reach their destination. Rhode Island's newly elected different governors responded that they knew nothing of these incidents because they had not been in situ as governors at the time. Investigations were promised, but the same conclusions were reached: unknown persons had been responsible. Infuriated, the British sent their own investigators with a reward equal to $2 million today. No one came forward. Hopkins, now a Chief Justice, argued that this British commission was illegal and that their presence on Rhode Island was unconstitutional. Rather rudely, he was told where to put his constitution. Hopkins wrote letters to all the colonies suggesting they unite against Britain. Few listened but, determined, he arranged a meeting in Philadelphia in September 1774 and called it a 'Continental Congress'.

Meanwhile, the British sent another ship. HMS *Rose*. She arrived at Rhode Island on 12 December 1774. Her captain, James Wallace's orders: put an end to the smuggling.

Because of the efficiency of her captain and crew, within a few weeks of *Rose*'s arrival the rum industry ceased. Thousands became unemployed. Wallace's presence was intolerable. To retaliate, the General Assembly re-established a Rhode Island Colonial Navy on 12 June 1775. Three days later, their two sloops, *Katy*, commanded by Abraham Whipple, and the *Washington*, chartered from Providence merchant John Brown, managed to capture a British sloop, *Diana*, which was patrolling Narragansett Bay. The first ship to be taken by the embryonic American Navy.

The Rhode Island General Assembly realised it would take more marine power to dislodge Wallace, so urged Congress to establish a proper navy on 26 August 1775, when Stephen Hopkins brought a Bill to create a Continental Navy of a mere two ships. With support from John Adams and John Hancock, a notorious smuggler, the Bill was passed on 13 October 1775. The Continental Navy was officially afloat.

Ships had to be found and refitted, crews had to be gathered. They eventually gained thirty ships and come the spring, sailed for Newport, with *Rose* as the target. Except, with smuggling ended *Rose*

HMS *Rose* – the scourge of the Rhode Island smugglers. The replica ship is now known as HMS *Surprise*, and also the author's own fictional *Sea Witch*.
(©RCP Photo)

had departed for Canada – the Americans had missed her by a few hours. Nevertheless, the Rhode Island General Assembly decided that no British ships were to have any further legal right to return, and to ensure this, Rhode Island declared independence from Great Britain on 4 May 1776, two months before the rest of the American Colonies.

But, I hear you ask, what about the episode that most people think started the War of Independence? That famous tea party at Boston Harbour?

The British Parliament passed a Revenue Act in 1767, which added three pence to every pound of tea exported to the American Colonies; in response, many Americans drank untaxed coffee instead, a tradition that is widely upheld today. Two years after the law was passed, tea was still being consumed by the teapot full, but it was provided by the smugglers who were plugging the gaping holes in the tax-levied tea-strainer. Because smuggling was hitting the tea trade, the East India Company sent an appeal for financial relief to the British Parliament.

The Tea Act of May 1773 enabled the East India Company to adjust import duties in their favour, and therefore benefit the company's finances and trade position in India. This meant that the Company could undersell the smugglers' prices in the Colonies. As Benjamin Franklin said, by importing cheap tea the British were attempting to, 'overcome all the patriotism of an American'.

Selecting a few designated ports, Charleston, New York, Philadelphia and Boston, in September 1773 the East India Company shipped 500,000lbs of tea across the Atlantic. The American Patriot groups refused to accept the shipments, but the Boston merchants would not agree with this pressure from the Patriots. The *Dartmouth* reached Boston on 27 November with the other two ships dropping anchor soon after. Meetings were held with the demand that the cargo was to be immediately returned to England – duty unpaid. Tempers flared, and on 16 December 1773 the final straw was reached. Disguised as Mohawk Indians and led by Samuel Adams, the Sons of Liberty forced their way aboard the three ships in Boston Harbour and destroyed 342 chests of tea by throwing them overboard. Three

US commemorative stamp featuring the events of the Boston Tea Party. (©Laufer)

hours later forty-five tons of tea was floating in the water, at a financial loss by today's standards of $1 million.

The British Government saw this insubordination as rebellion and responded by closing Boston Harbour and passing punitive measures against the Massachusetts Colony – which poured oil on a fire that was already well-lit. Twelve colonies combined to form the Continental Congress in order to coordinate resistance and effectively seized independent rule. George Washington was appointed by Congress to command the Continental Army and the ensuing fighting was brutal and prolonged, but at the end of it all America won independence. And all that because of smuggling contraband!

Little Known Fact:
There were two 'tea parties' – not just
the one at Boston.

The Boston Tea Party is known as the significant act of defiance that turned the tide for American Independence, but who has heard of the Philadelphia Tea Party of December, 1773?

Similar to events in Boston, Philadelphia held a town meeting at the Pennsylvania State House, now known as Independence House, on 16 October 1773. The meeting was arranged by several prominent figures and notable men of the Philadelphia Sons of Liberty Patriots. Echoing Benjamin Franklin, one of the eighteen resolutions they agreed was, 'That the duty imposed by Parliament upon tea landed in America is a tax on the Americans, or levying contributions on them without their consent.' Even more important was the agreement: 'The resolution lately entered into by the East India Company, to send out their tea to America subject to the payment of duties on its being landed here, is an open attempt to enforce the ministerial plan, and a violent attack upon the liberties of America.'

The declaration published in the *Pennsylvania Gazette* was the first publicly acclaimed protest against imported tea from England and was, therefore, a statement of rebellion against George III. The events of Boston happened a mere three weeks later, with Bostonians adopting more-or-less the same declaration.

But the unrest against the import of tea did not end at Boston, or with subversive (in the view of the British) declarations. On Christmas Day 1773, the ship, *Polly*, commanded by Captain Ayres and carrying a cargo of 697 chests of tea, sailed up the Delaware River bound for Chester, Pennsylvania and *James & Drinker*, a Philadelphia Quaker firm.

Polly was intercepted and escorted to drop anchor in Philadelphia Harbour; 8,000 citizens of the city met two days later to discuss what to do next. Several resolutions were proposed and agreed, the main one being that the tea should not be brought ashore. The *Polly* was to sail back down the Delaware and be gone. Undoubtedly, Captain Ayres agreed because otherwise the consequences, made quite clear to him, would be undesirable. Likewise, the company expecting to receive the tea was given similar warnings. Ayres duly went back aboard his ship, re-provisioned with fresh food and water and returned to England, with the cargo of tea.

This peaceful result was due to the influence of the Quakers. Ayres had even been staying in a harbour-side inn – all expenses paid.

But who would have thought that a bid to stop the annoyance of smugglers would result in an entire country gaining independence, to the abandonment of sovereignty and a king, and to the inauguration of a president – General George Washington.

PUNISHMENT FOR THE CRIME

Chapter Eighteen

Did it All End at the Gallows?

I t is doubtful that trading in illegal goods will ever be effectively stopped, but for our smugglers time was running out... If a smuggler was caught, prior to the late eighteenth century, the penalty was death by hanging, but by the 1800s the humanitarian attitude (such as it debatably was) behind sentencing and punishments was starting to change. Was the hangman's noose always the expectation of a smuggler's fate?

Depending on the time period, a smuggler who had been caught, arrested and sent to trial faced the prospect of the noose, the dreadful conditions of the prison hulks, or transportation to Australia, but these were not always a foregone conclusion. Even when imprisoned, many, especially the leaders and those with higher responsibilities, had the wherewithal to bully or bribe a jury – even a magistrate or judge – to bring in a 'not guilty' verdict. Nor was there any hesitation in using violence in any suitable form against individuals or their family members to ensure the end result was a not guilty verdict. These were lawless times anyway, and when the life or freedom of one of their own was at stake, the gangs knew how to deal with the situation and ensure the longevity of their trusted and loyal colleagues.

Fines were another option, but in the early days it was possible to request a trial rather than merely pay-up if caught. John Rogers of Dorset was one such plaintiff. Suspected of wool smuggling in 1428 he asked for a trial in preference to paying a demanded fine. The Privy Council denied his request citing that a jury would be local men who were likely to acquit the charge, even with the irrefutable evidence to bring a guilty verdict. Rogers was therefore commanded to pay the fixed fine of 200 marks, or more if he could afford it.

I wonder, did he admit that he could afford more, or did he, prudently, keep quiet?

Little Known Fact:
If weight was added to the dangling unfortunate, death
came quicker, so to speed up the process, family and
friends would 'hang on' to the victim's legs and torso.
Which is where the term 'hangers on' comes from.

The word is 'hanged' for people, not 'hung' as in putting up curtains, such are the vagaries of the English language for ne'er-do-wells unfortunate enough to be sentenced to death. Hanging was an unpleasant business, but drew great crowds of onlookers to gawp at the spectacle. A hanging day was akin to a festival; out would come the hawkers and sellers, the prostitutes and the cutpurses, for a hanging day was a day when the town would be packed with people. Before the introduction of the 'long drop with the sudden stop' the procedure could take up to twenty minutes for the victim to die, slowly strangling to death.

In London, the most famous places of execution were Tyburn, near the current position of Marble Arch; Tower Hill close to the Tower of London and Wapping alongside the river Thames – which was especially used for dispatching pirates. Captain Kidd was hanged here in May 1701, and was unfortunate enough to suffer the trauma of the rope snapping – twice. Had it given way a third time he would have been regarded as innocent in the eyes of God and reprieved. Alas for Kidd, the third time that he was 'pushed off' was the final time.

Public executions had the purpose of discouraging crime by demonstrating the power of the law to those tempted to break it. The Tyburn hangings took place eight times a year, and were supposed to be conducted in a sombre manner in order to enhance the severity of the punishment. The festival atmosphere rather undermined that intention.

Calls for the death penalty to be made more humane came in the 1770s, but not until 1868 did public hangings cease in favour of execution within the privacy of the prison, while the 'drop' gallows, via a trapdoor opening, was first used at Newgate in 1783. The rope was knotted and set so that the neck was broken and the jugular vein ruptured as the drop is made; not necessarily painless nor a quicker way to die – there were instances of the head being ripped clean off.

The situation of overcrowding in London and other towns, and the subsequent increase in crime, particularly theft, caused major problems for the British Government. A solution was to use old ships, discarded after various wars, as floating prisons anchored in the Thames and other major rivers, or offshore at certain coastal areas. There were about forty of these derelict hulks converted for such use.

Conditions aboard were appalling: disease, no sanitation and poor food, foul water and little air or light. The decks were riddled with vermin. It is estimated that 11,000 men and women died on these hulks – more souls than soldiers killed in the American War of Independence. For many of the hulks, depending on where they were moored, the heat was intense in summer or freezing in winter.

The first vessel acquired by the government in 1775 was intended as temporary accommodation due to the disruption of transportation of convicts to the Americas because of the outbreak of war. Many of the first arrivals accepted pardons in exchange for joining the army or navy. They made the right choice.

Prison hulks appear in fiction, most notably *Great Expectations* by Charles Dickens, which opens with the escape of Magwitch in 1812 from a hulk moored in the Thames Estuary, although in reality most of the ships were in the Medway, not the Thames. Jean Valjean in Victor Hugo's *Les Misérables*, is a convict held on the prison hulks at Toulon, France.

Full beyond capacity, prison hulks could take no more convicts, hanging was abating, except for murder and rape, so using the newly discovered continent of Australia seemed an ideal solution to the overcrowding problem. Prior to Captain Cook's initial voyages of discovery, it is estimated that at least sixty thousand indentured, or forced labour, white convicts had been sent to work in the Americas. The War of Independence put an end to that particular form of slavery, but between 1788 and 1868 over 160,000 more were transported to Australia.

Eleven convict ships sailed for Botany Bay in 1787, dropping anchor in January 1788. The initial landing place proved unsuitable, so an alternative was found and the harbour named after Viscount Sydney, the Home Secretary responsible for using Australia as a penal colony. Peaking in the 1830s the last convict ship arrived in January 1868.

Transportation was regarded as more humane than hanging, but there was an extremely high death rate among those first convicts because of disease and food shortages – the ships did not carry enough to sustain the settlement until agriculture and livestock could be established, along with a lack of experienced farmers. The second fleet to arrive in June 1790 increased the problem. Perhaps hanging would have been a better option than starvation?

Was the law effective against smuggling? The risk of being caught and punished was a small one, and in the first half of the eighteenth century lawbreaking increased because of Jacobite support for exiled James II, III and 'Bonnie Prince Charlie'. More than one of the notorious gangs were Jacobites. Legislation followed legislation in order to crack down on the Trade. The Hovering Act of 1718/19 made it illegal for small vessels to wait at anchor if within six miles of the coast. Any boat found carrying something it should not was seized and destroyed, but proving 'hovering' was not easy. Captains merely stated that they were waiting for a favourable wind or tide.

Little Known Fact:
A law was passed to make it illegal to use more than four oars in a rowing boat.

In Kent and Essex it became illegal to use more than four oars to row a boat. Anyone caught loitering, carrying firearms, or hiding his face by use of a scarf could be arrested and sent for transportation. The laws were ineffective – smuggling tactics merely changed.

An attempt to offer arrested smugglers free pardons in return for naming names resulted in endangering the lives of kindred and damage to property. The 1736 Act of Indemnity merely increased the violence from the smuggling gangs. Transportation for resisting arrest along with the death penalty if preventative officers were injured meant that murder became more common. Dead men, after all, tell no tales.

In 1746 yet more legislations were passed, and again failed. Hanging was extended to cover anyone found guilty of having anything to do with smuggling. The conflict with the Americas in 1776 drained government troops, leaving few behind in Britain to patrol the coasts as preventative men. Taxes went up, law enforcement came down. More discussion was made in the 1780s when smuggling took another substantial increase. The revenue cutters and crews were hopelessly outnumbered. Finally, an enquiry came up with a solution. At last it was realised that if goods did not carry such a high duty there would be nothing of value to smuggle. In 1784 William Pitt cut the import duty on tea from 129 per cent to 12½ per cent. Instantly tea was unprofitable as contraband. Unfortunately, this enlightenment did not extend to other commodities, and smuggling continued for many other goods.

A Martello Tower, built to protect the south coast against possible invasion by the French during the Napoleonic Wars. Once redundant, the blockade men used them as watchtowers to keep an eye on smuggling activity. (©dazb75)

The French Revolution opened its first disruption in 1792 and continued through to 1803, and then the Napoleonic Wars lasted until 1815. Men were taken from the preventative services and smuggling flourished again by trading with the French.

Prior to Nelson's victory at Trafalgar, where Napoleon's fleet was destroyed, a French invasion was expected. Defences were built along southern English coasts in the form of Martello Towers. Designed as lookout posts, they proved to be more of an inconvenience to the smugglers than they were to the French.

For England, the law succeeded eventually because the gangs became so violent that public support for what used to be seen as harmless, changed. Opinion turned against the smugglers, and once that happened the Trade was doomed. By 1809 the Preventative Waterguard had been established, cutters and rowing boats were being used by the revenue men, enabling access to rivers and shallower bays along the coast. Their pay was increased, which in turn raised morale. When the Coast Blockade marched into Kent and Sussex and took up residence in the Martello Towers, it all seemed to be over for the Free Trade. Bribery was common, under-manning was still a problem, but the days of 'five-and-twenty ponies trotting through the dark' were rapidly drawing to a close.

FACT AND FICTION?

Chapter Nineteen

Escape into a Novel

C an smuggling fit in with any type of story? As a plot-mechanic, it is a good theme for adventures, mysteries, thrillers and historical fiction, but fiction is not intended to be interpreted as fact. The aim of fiction is to entertain. Before the nastier side of smuggling came to the fore, drug and human trafficking in particular, the 'Trade of Gentleman' was highlighted by romantic works of fiction, some concentrating on smuggling as a main plot, others with smaller, but essential, scenes. Very few of both, however, portrayed anything near the reality, but then, does that matter?

Most twenty-first century authors of historical fiction are careful to ensure they have their facts right, for one small but well-known incorrect blooper can result in social-media ridicule, the story being ruined for readers and the author tarnished by poor credibility. A Roman Centurion enjoying a pipe of tobacco while on watch on Hadrian's Wall, for instance, is utter nonsense – tobacco was not introduced into England until after the Americas were 'discovered' by Columbus when he 'sailed the ocean blue in fourteen-hundred and ninety-two'. What would our smugglers have done without the money-making 'weed'! Fiction is fiction, but to be convincing with the made-up imaginative bits, an author has to take care that the factual bits *are* factual.

Smuggling, with its air of mystery, heroism and that all–important disregard of the law is, not surprisingly, an ideal theme for fiction, films and even opera.

James Bond occasionally uses his 'Licence to Kill' to thwart smuggling gangs in the movies adapted from Ian Fleming's novels. British author, Eric Clifford Ambler OBE wrote thrillers, and in particular, spy novels. His *The Light of Day*, published in 1962 was made into a successful movie in 1964 as *Topkapi*, which is about stealing a valuable emerald-encrusted dagger from a Turkish museum and smuggling it out of the country. All good, exciting stuff.

People smuggling is the basic plot of a series of adventures written by Baroness Orczy. The flower, the Scarlet Pimpernel, *Primulaceae: Anagallis Arvensis* is to many gardeners a weed, although it is actually a wild flower. It is also the trademark 'calling card' and pseudonym of Sir Percy Blakeney – *The Scarlet Pimpernel*. The stories are about his secretive mission to outwit the French by helping the aristocrats to escape the fate of the guillotine by smuggling them to the safety of England. Behind the fiction is the reality of the French Revolution, a period of social and political upheaval lasting from 1789 until 1799 and which caused global unrest throughout the Western World, mainly due to the fear by monarchs and governments that the Reign of Terror would spread. Factually, many of the nobility were smuggled from France to the safety of England, although many more met a terrible fate. In turn, the Revolution paved the way for the Napoleonic Wars which brought an increase in smuggling.

> We seek him here, we seek him there,
> Those Frenchies seek him everywhere.
> Is he in heaven? Is he in hell?
> That damned, elusive, Pimpernel.

People-smuggling also provided an exciting backdrop to *Underground To Canada* by Barbara Smucker (1915–2003). It is a young adult's passionate novel about the secret railroad used to smuggle escaped slaves from the American South into Canada.

Arthur Russell Thorndike (1885–1972) was a British actor who was not quite as well known as his actress sister, Dame Sybil Thorndike, but he was widely applauded for his *Doctor Syn* novels, which were about smuggling on Romney Marsh.

The first in the series, *Doctor Syn: A Tale of the Romney Marsh* was published in 1915 and soon became popular, although possibly a

The scarlet pimpernel. (©Paul – Adobe Stock)

little old-fashioned for the taste of modern readers. Following several adventures Dr Syn is offered the position of vicar of Dymchurch. He hopes for a peaceful life, but soon realises that his parish is steeped in smuggling and that his parishioners are in danger of being discovered by the excise men. The only way he can help is to use his wits, intelligence and position as a respectable vicar and to become the smuggling gang's leader.

Being one of the major smuggling areas, there are quite a few novels set around the rugged and remote Cornish and Devon coasts and moors. The Doones of Exmoor, featured in R.D. Blackmore's fictional tale, *Lorna Doone*, were notorious thieves and smugglers, while one of the most famous, as we have already discovered when we stopped there for a tot of smuggled brandy, is *Jamaica Inn* by Daphne du Maurier, but Cornwall can boast a handsome fictional hero who, for a while at least, turned to the Free Trade to keep the wolf – or rather his neighbour, George Warleggan – from the door.

The *Poldark* series by Winston Graham has been a favourite of historical fiction readers for many years, well before the two highly popular TV series came to our screens. Published originally between 1945 and 1953, then continuing from 1973 to 2002, there are twelve novels set in Cornwall from 1783 to 1820.

Little Known Fact:
Winston Graham initially named his lead character
Ross 'Polgreen' – but changed it to Poldark.

The series follows Captain Ross Poldark's misfortunes and fortunes; his struggle to avoid debt and to come to terms with life and love.

His counterpart is rich banker, George Warleggan, who is determined to be respected as the new aristocracy. As his wealth increases, so does his contempt for the poor – and Ross. The tension between Ross's desire to assist the mining community and George's obsession with attempting to ruin Ross financially, and morally, forms much of the backbone of the drama. But what about the smuggling?

Early in the series Ross is accused of wrecking, for which he is acquitted, but facing bankruptcy he is then drawn into a series of smuggling runs, and it is these highly dramatic, nail-biting and superbly accurate scenes that set the tone of eighteenth-century life in a Cornish coastal community struggling to survive.

Author Winston Graham researched the history with meticulous care; tin mining, medical knowledge, the horror of Bodmin Jail, the poverty, the snobbery of the upper classes – particularly when Enclosures deprived families of the use of common land, and the Corn Laws added to the misery of starvation. In the later books, parliamentary reform, the coming of the Industrial Revolution and the building of the railways add to the social impact portrayed. All of which were valid influences for supporting the Free Trade.

Surprisingly, Charles Dickens did not use smuggling in his novels, even though his favourite residence was situated at Broadstairs, overlooking all the busy maritime activity along the Kent coast. His home there, Fort House, was built in 1801, although we know it by the name it was given in 1870, Bleak House. Either Mr Dickens was a stickler for the law or perhaps he kept quiet because he knew one

or two smugglers and had a useful cellar? We can only surmise....
Thomas Hardy, however, had direct personal experience of
smuggling! Between the years 1801–05, that great and well-respected
author of *Far From the Madding Crowd* and *Tess of the d'Urbervilles*,
bore witness to his grandfather indulging in a spot of smuggling.
Grandfather's Wessex house was a secluded one, and according to
Hardy's notebooks, the elderly gentleman occasionally kept as many
as eighty tubs of smuggled liquor in a closet beneath a staircase.
Hardy wrote:

> The tubs, or little elongated barrels, were of thin staves
> with wooden hoops. They were brought at night by men
> on horseback, 'slung' or in carts. A whiplash across the
> windowpane would wake my grandfather at two or three
> in the morning, and he would dress and go down. Not a
> soul was there, but a heap of tubs loomed up in front of
> the door. He would set to work and stow them in the dark
> closet aforesaid, and nothing more would happen till dusk
> the following evening, when groups of dark, long-bearded
> fellows would arrive, and carry off the tubs slung over their
> shoulders.

Clearly, young Master Hardy was not 'watching the wall' when the
'Gentlemen went by'!

Hardy's *Wessex Tales* mention smuggling, while in his *The
Distracted Preacher* we have these delightful lines:

> 'Not smugglers' liquor?' he said.
> 'Yes,' said she. 'They are tubs of spirit that have accidentally
> come over in the dark from France.'

In novels, movies, poem and art, smuggling has been a popular theme,
although not as popular as those dastardly knaves, the pirates. Novels
such as *Jamaica Inn* and *Moonfleet* romanticised the Trade, while for
their acclaimed paintings famous artists courted the lure of a moonlit
night, the call of the sea and the Gentlemen setting about their secretive

business. *Folkestone From the Sea*, *Twilight – Smugglers off Folkestone Fishing Up Smuggled Gin* and *Folkestone, Kent*, are paintings produced in the 1820s by Turner depicting smuggling in highly accurate detail. It has been suggested that Turner must have accompanied the smugglers to see first-hand what went on and how, as inspiration for his chosen subjects. He visited Folkestone in 1821, so the conjecture is feasible. But does fiction portray an authentic view of the exploits of the real smugglers of the past?

Probably not, but then, that is why it is entitled 'fiction'.

Chapter Twenty

Them that ask no Questions isn't
Told a Lie

Will our fascination, even respect and admiration, for smugglers ever diminish? Smuggling, in the past affected almost everyone, one way or another. The difference between then and now is that modern-day smuggling is more sinister than 'The Trade' of the seventeenth and eighteenth centuries. Today's drugs, guns, ivory, exotic animals and desperate people, are the money-makers for those with a get-rich-quick, no conscience or morals agenda. Not to say that the smuggled brandy and tobacco of the past do not count as harmless commodities, but in comparison to the twenty-first century, smuggling in the days of the 1700–1800s was relatively benign.

Or was it? As we have seen, it seems, probably not. The image of the lone Ross Poldark-type figure on that isolated Cornish beach, whistling jauntily as he hauls in his boat, then lugs a keg of contraband brandy across the sun-baked golden sand and up the cliff path to his cosy cottage belongs almost entirely to fiction. The fact of smuggling is that most of it was organised by vicious gangs who would as soon cut your throat as pass you a packet of 'baccy.

Smuggling today continues, with the methods becoming more devious and the Customs and Excise using more and more advanced technology to combat the twenty-first century Free Traders, each group determined to outsmart the other, but smuggling will never be completely brought to order, not as long as goods are in demand, sold on for a cheaper price and there are people willing to risk imprisonment – or even their life – to earn an 'easy' profit.

The admiration we possess comes to us entirely through fiction, TV and movies. In our novels we read about the handsome hero getting the better of the baddies, or watch on screen the lithe figure risking all, facing horrors and dangers but triumphing in the end. Who remembers a certain chocolate box advertisement where the man smuggles into a bedroom a box of chocs, then whisks off, silent as a shadow, into the night – and all because 'the lady loves Milk Tray'?

The unexpected hero of the original *Star Wars* movies, before the franchise ended up with the producer-only-knows how many additional episodes and spin-offs were to be included, was supposed to have been Luke Skywalker but Han Solo took centre stage – the rugged smuggler, not the young Jedi Knight.

Although pirates, not smugglers, the same happened in the Disney Franchise *Pirates Of The Caribbean*, Will Turner was the intended heart-throb hero, but he was firmly made to walk the plank by Jack Sparrow, pirate captain and smuggler.

Were the men and women – and children – in those quiet middle-of-nowhere villages of Cornwall, Devon, Kent or Sussex, admirers of the smugglers? On the whole, yes they were, for the simple fact that many of those items of illicit contraband were lifesavers, especially when the items were corn or salt. Maybe minds were changed, however, when the apparent heroes became the bad guy villains?

But the Gentlemen were soon to become bygone heroes, for by the mid-1840s a free-trade policy was introduced by Parliament, which effectively brought all import duties down to a more sensible level, although what is sensible can be disputed by some people where Customs and Excise are concerned. Within a decade of that parliamentary decision large-scale smuggling of the items that had been classed as luxury goods, and the smuggling gangs that made a living from smuggling them, had become consigned to where they remain today, on movie or TV screens, or on the pages of tales of imagined fiction.

But I will leave you with this thought: